A HISTORY OF WOMEN'S LIVES IN
SCUNTHORPE

With best wishes

Carole McTx

A HISTORY OF WOMEN'S LIVES IN
SCUNTHORPE

BY CAROLE McENTEE TAYLOR

PEN & SWORD
HISTORY

AN IMPRINT OF PEN & SWORD BOOKS LTD.
YORKSHIRE · PHILADELPHIA

First published in Great Britain in 2019 by
Pen & Sword HISTORY
An imprint of
Pen & Sword Books Limited
Yorkshire - Philadelphia

ISBN 978 1 52671 7 177

A CIP catalogue record for this book is available from the British Library

Printed and bound in the UK
by TJ International Ltd, Padstow, Cornwall

Typeset in 11.5/14 point Times New Roman
by Aura Technology and Software Services, India

Pen & Sword Books Limited incorporates the imprints of Atlas,
Archaeology, Aviation, Discovery, Family History, Fiction, History, Maritime,
Military, Military Classics, Politics, Select, Transport, True Crime, Air World,
Frontline Publishing, Leo Cooper, Remember When, Seaforth Publishing,
The Praetorian Press, Wharncliffe Local History, Wharncliffe Transport,
Wharncliffe True Crime and White Owl.

For a complete list of Pen & Sword titles please contact
PEN & SWORD BOOKS LIMITED
47 Church Street, Barnsley, South Yorkshire S70 2AS, United Kingdom
E-mail: enquiries@pen-and-sword.co.uk
Website: www.pen-and-sword.co.uk

Or
PEN AND SWORD BOOKS
1950 Lawrence Rd, Havertown, PA 19083, USA
E-mail: Uspen-and-sword@casematepublishers.com
Website: www.penandswordbooks.com

Contents

Acknowledgements

I would first like to thank the Helen Marris Collection very much for the use of the Co-operative Society and the Scunthorpe Church of England School (later known as Gurnell Street School) material and Bryan Longbone for all his help. I would also like to thank Eddie Baker who provided many of the photos and to say how sorry I am that he didn't live to see the book. Last, but not least, I would like to thank Maureen and Kevin Hempsall for the information and photos relating to Rose Peake.

In January 1907, Florence Booth, the daughter-in-law of William Booth, the founder of the Salvation Army asked if she could start a women's organisation within the Salvation Army. On 28 January the Home League was formed to promote the redemption of family life. I would like to thank the Salvation Army in Ashby for allowing me to speak to women during their coffee mornings and also to Ruth Boswell for telling me about the Home League and for introducing me to so many ladies from the Ashby Home League.

Last, but certainly not least, I would like to thank all the ladies who kindly spared me a few moments of their time and shared their memories with me.

Introduction

A History of Women's Lives in Scunthorpe shines a brief spotlight on the lives of over 150 women who lived in Scunthorpe between 1842 and 1950 and mentions a similar number by name. It is not an in-depth social study of inequality or suffrage, or a feminist manifesto. It does not concentrate on the lives of women with money, although they are mentioned, nor are there pages of social history and explanations as to why society viewed women in certain ways. Instead the book sets out to offer a snapshot of different aspects of the lives of ordinary women and to show, through personal memories and examples taken from the time, that although in some ways things have changed dramatically, in others society has not really progressed at all.

Although the women come from Scunthorpe, the morals and norms of society that can be seen through court decisions and other aspects of their lives could probably be taken from anywhere in the country.

CHAPTER ONE

The Beginning 1842 – 1900

Scunthorpe began life as one of five villages overlooking the Trent Valley, its name originating from an old Danish word Escumetorp. Ashby, Brumby, Crosby, Frodingham and Scunthorpe had less than a mile between them. In 1824, the first edition of the Ordnance Survey for the area describes Scunthorpe as little more than a country lane with a few white-washed cottages and farm houses.

However, the area was not entirely crime free. On Sunday, 1 May 1842, someone broke into the draper's and grocer shop of Elizabeth Borman and stole a number of silk handkerchiefs, some green with red sprigs and others chocolate coloured. They also stole three pieces of fancy gauze ribbon, some bonnet ribbon, a ham, some pocket knives and various other items. The Ashby Association for the Prosecution of Felons offered a ten guinea reward for information leading to the capture of the burglar. The notice also stated that if the theft had been carried out by two people and one of them reported their accomplice to the authorities, that person would also receive the reward money.

Four years later, on 3 August, Elizabeth's shop was broken into again. Several shawls, silk handkerchiefs, pieces of habit cloth, ribbons and muslin were stolen. But this time the perpetrator was arrested. On 14 August 1846, James Drayton was charged with burglary at Elizabeth Borman's shop in Scunthorpe. Some of the goods were recovered and James Drayton was remanded.

Scunthorpe did not change very much over the next few years and by 1851 the population was just 303 with 113 people living in

Frodingham, 46 in Brumby, 214 in Crosby and 456 in Ashby. This would change after the discovery of iron ore by Roland Winn on his father's land near Scunthorpe. In July 1860, the first ore was mined and two years later an iron works was built. Enoch Markham, a fitter at the Trent Iron Works, came to Scunthorpe from Mexborough. He helped to fit up the first furnace at the works and the cottages there were built for him and the other workers to live in. At this time Scunthorpe still had only two shops with a few scattered houses in between.

Eleven years later the population of Scunthorpe had risen to 616 and that of Frodingham to 577. The number of people living in the other three villages had also changed. While Ashby now had a population of 669 and Crosby 288, Frodingham and Brumby's population had actually declined from 204 to 178. Scunthorpe had a chemist, a surgeon, a resident police sergeant, an ironmonger, a mining engineer and mining agent. Of the 616 people on the census, 94 had been born outside Lincolnshire.

Mary Frances Skinner was born in 1854 in Scunthorpe to William and Ann Skinner. William was a wheelwright and carpenter. Mary was the oldest of three children and had a younger brother, Alfred (b.1856) and two sisters, Ann (b.1858) and Rose (b.1860). Robert Lees (b.1843) was a foreman of the furnace labourers. He lived in Park Street, Scunthorpe but came from Dukinfield in Cheshire. Mary married Robert in 1869. They had one daughter Ann (b.1871) and four sons, James (b.1873), Robert (b.1880), Albert (b.1884) and Charles (b.1889). On 22 July 1890, Robert was working in Ashton-under-Lyne as a miner in Nook, Rowley for Broad Oak Colliery Company when he was killed in an accident. According to the colliery records he was suffocated by gas and coal dust. Mary had just discovered that she was pregnant again and gave birth to her fifth son, Frederick Ellis on 7 April 1891. Ann was living with her uncle William and Aunt Alice in Dukinfield, Cheshire, James was a farm labourer, Robert and Albert were at school and Mary had taken in a lodger, Charles Crackles, a farm labourer aged 43. A few years later Mary moved to 57 South Street and was working as a charwoman. James continued to live at home and was still a farm labourer. By the time Mary Lees was 60 years of age she was working as a farm labourer in Scotter. James, now 40, and Fred, aged 20, were both single and living with Mary, their occupations also listed as farm labourers.

In May 1870, Emma Middleton summoned John Thomas Toine, a farm servant from Brumby, to court to ask for maintenance for her illegitimate child. An order was made for 1s 6d per week from birth, 17s 6d costs and 10s for the midwife.

At the Winterton Petty Sessions in February 1876 William Cockles, Samuel Gillat and Thomas Johnson from Scunthorpe were fined 10s each and ordered to pay 12s 6d costs for an unprovoked assault on Lucy Armitage, also from Scunthorpe, on 10 February.

By 1881, the population of Scunthorpe had risen to 2,126 and four years later there were two women grocers in the village – Maria Waters and Sarah Ann Holt.

Sarah Ann Holt (née Brown) was born in Keadby on 11 July 1830 to James and Sarah Brown (née Davey). Sarah had an older sister Mary (b.1828), younger sisters, Hannah (b.1833) and Elizabeth (b.1840) and younger brothers, John (b.1835), William (b.1838) and James (b.1845). James was an agricultural labourer in 1841, but later became a school teacher.

Sarah married William Holt, a bricklayer, on 23 May 1859 at Althorpe. The couple already had a son, Uriah (b.1855) and went on to have seven more children, James (b.1860), Sarah (b.1862), Hannah (b.1864), Clara (b.1865), John (b.1868), Frank (b.1870) and William (1872–75). Six years later the family were living in Ashby and Sarah had a grocer and draper's shop. James was now a weighman and clerk, Sarah was a servant in Doncaster, Hannah was a general domestic servant but living at home. The other boys were still at school. Sarah died on 22 March 1899.

Elizabeth Sowden was born in Gunhouse, Lincoln in 1839 to Abraham and Mary Sowden (née Bainton) and was baptised in February 1840. Elizabeth was the oldest child and had a brother Enoch (b.1845) and sister Jane (b.1847). By the age of 21 Elizabeth was estranged from her family and living in the workhouse in Brigg. Two years later she married William Carlisle on 25 December 1863.

The couple had eight children, John Thomas (b.1865), Mary Jane (b.1867), George Lewis (b.1868) Alfred Charles (b.1870), William Henry (b.1872), Sophia (b.1874), Arthur F. (b.1877) and Walter A. (b.1878).

By 1888, Elizabeth, aged 47, had been ill for some time with heart disease and she died in August. In 1911 at the age of 70, William was living in the workhouse in Brigg.

Steel manufacturing began in Frodingham in 1890 and, as agricultural workers came in from the surrounding villages and skilled workers came from other areas in the country, the population in the villages grew rapidly. In 1891, Frodingham had a population of 1,384 but the fastest growth was in Scunthorpe which had reached urban district status in 1883 and by 1891 the population had risen to 3,417.

Roland Winn, now Lord St Oswald, gave St John's Church to the town and it opened in 1891. The church only had only one bell but seven more were provided through public money as a memorial when Roland died in 1893. The Primitive Methodist Church in Scunthorpe High Street also opened in 1891. It was knocked down to build British Home Stores in the 1960s.

Frodingham Sunday School 1890.

Bluebell Laundry Girls 1890.

The Annual Scunthorpe Statutes for hiring servants were held on 17 May 1892. The Scunthorpe Statutes were becoming well known as one of the best in the area and were well attended. Housemaids were hired for between £10 – £14 per annum (p.a.); the wages for general servants were between £9 – £12 p.a. Milking girls were very scarce but those who were there were engaged for £11 15s p.a. Manservants and waggoners' wages ranged from £16 – £22 p.a.; second horsemen £12 – £16 p.a. and boys £7 – £9 p.a.

Rose Hannah Peake was born on 30 January 1894 to

Walter and Bertha Peake, parents of Rosie Hannah Peake.

Rosie Hannah Peake.

Walter (1861 – 1940) and Bertha Peake (née Kime) (1862 – 1935). Walter was an agricultural foreman and he and Bertha lived at 28 Ermine Street. Ten years later Walter was a farm foreman and still at 28 Ermine Street. Also living in the house with Walter, Bertha and Rosie were four servants: Frank Westoby, aged 21; William Hunsley aged 20; Corney Standerline aged 17 and Arthur Hunsley aged 16. In the years leading up to the Great War the family remained in the same house, but the servants had moved on. Now living with them were 21-year-old Harry Scott, a waggoner on the farm; 20-year-old Fred Hartley, another waggoner; 18-year-old Herbert Standlim, the houseman and 16-year-old William Wynne, another houseman. When the war started Rosie began writing to several servicemen, including some of the servants who had worked on the farm. She wrote so many postcards and letters that the local post office sent her Christmas cards.

Rosie's cousin, Stanley Barley, was born on 1 June 1889 to William Barley (b.1860) and Jane Ellen Peake (1863 – 1948). Stanley enlisted into the East Yorkshire Regiment (East Yorks) in Grimsby and was given the regimental number 151710. He transferred to the Machine Gun Corps, was given the new number 63701 and promoted to serjeant. Stanley died of his wounds on 24 October 1918.

Its likely that through her cousin Stanley, Rosie met Harry John Sharman to whom she later became engaged. Harry was born on 11 January 1892 in Lodden, Norfolk to John (b.1863) and Martha Emily Sharman (née Blazer b.1866). He was baptised on

Stanley Barley, Rosie's cousin.

Left: *Private Harry John Sharman, Rosie's boyfriend.*

Below: *Front of postcard from Harry to Rosie.*

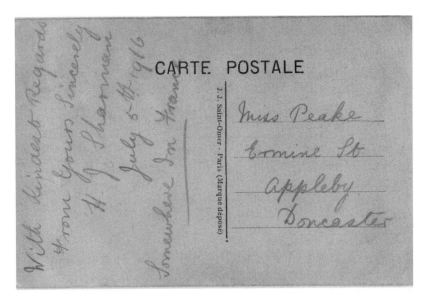

Back of postcard to Rosie from Harry.

15 February 1892 in Claxton, Norfolk. At the beginning of the twentieth century Harry, aged 9, was living with his parents and older brother 10-year-old George and younger sisters 7-year-old Lilian and 2-year-old Ethel.

Harry was a teamster of horses and went to France sometime after the beginning of 1916. He was originally in the East Yorkshire Regiment (no.20140) and later transferred to the 55th Battalion Machine Gun Corps, and given a new number 14175. Harry was killed in action on 5 May 1918.

After Harry's death Rosie continued to write to the soldiers at the front and these included Private Edgar William Donner (330928) who was born in Morton, Lincolnshire about 1900 to Edgar Donner (1870 –1948) and Susan Maplethorpe (b.1878). Edgar was previously in the 8th Battalion East Yorkshire Regiment (1347) and the 13th Royal Scots (271545). He was also with 4th Reserve Battalion, C Coy, Royal Scots. Whilst in the 13th Service Battalion Edgar contracted impetigo on 6 November 1918. He was soon pronounced fit for duty and went back to the front the next day. Edgar died in December 1949.

Private Edgar
William
Donner.

Rosie never married. She spent the rest of her years collecting postcards and writing to friends and relatives. She died on 5 February 1977 aged 83 and is buried in St Bartholmew Church cemetery Appelby.

By 1895, Scunthorpe was growing in industrial importance. Ironmaking was well established, but despite the rapid growth in the town there was no magistrates court and petty sessions were

28 Ermine Street, the house Rosie lived in.

held at Winterton. Scunthorpe did have a police station with one sergeant and four constables, but they came under a superintendent who was based in Winterton.

There was, however, a new Urban District Council. The first council elections took place on 17 December 1894. There were forty-five candidates chasing fifteen places, but Scunthorpe only had one seat on Lindsey County Council – Councillor J. Foster. Most women did not have a vote although they were involved in politics.

On Wednesday, 28 February 1896, the Scunthorpe and Frodingham Women's Liberal Federation held a business meeting followed by a tea and meeting that was open to everyone in the public hall. Mrs Jarvis presided and there were several speakers including Countess Alice Kearny, Mrs Douse, Mrs Hornsby, Mrs Barkworth (Winterton) Councillor Fletcher and the Revs. S. Cutts and W. Scruby.

In 1896, Mr and Mrs Jackson of Scunthorpe adopted a little girl from the Brigg workhouse. Every attempt had been made to find the girl's mother before the adoption went ahead, but the Guardians had no success. The Jacksons loved the child and were very happy until the arrival of a Syrian woman, who claimed she was the girl's paternal grandmother and that the child should return to Syria with her. The Jacksons begged the woman that they should be allowed to keep the girl, but the woman went to the Brigg Board of Guardians who listened to the story of how she had travelled thousands of miles to find her granddaughter and then ordered the Jacksons to give the child to her. The Jacksons still refused and the Board of Guardians were trying to decide what to do for the best when, in November of the same year, the mother suddenly reappeared. Mrs Florence Benson had been living at 5 Industrial Place, Norman Street in Lincoln when she had read about the case in the *Lincoln Reader* and realised this was her child. She immediately wrote to the Jacksons and sent a copy of her letter to the Board of Guardians.

The letter stated that she had been married and had left the child with the man she'd believed to be her husband, who was a photographer in Retford and that she had no idea he'd died until she read the report in the newspaper. (Joseph died in Hull in July 1896). Florence begged the Jacksons not to let the child go to Syria and arranged to meet them. She then signed a document giving all rights over the child to the Jacksons and told her story.

Mary Ellen (Florence) Wood was born on 4 February 1872 in Stapleford, Lincolnshire to George and Eliza Wood (née Cook). She had five older brothers, Henry (b.1863), Joell (b.1865), William (b.1866), David (b.1868) and George (b.1870) and six younger sisters Emma (b.1874), Rose (b.1875), Annie (b.1876), Bertha (b.1878), Sarah (b.1882 and Alice (b.1885).

She had met Joseph Neumeyer in America, fallen in love with him and married in America – at least she had presumed they were married as the service had been in French. Joseph set up his business as a photographer in New York and the marriage seemed happy. On 6 February 1895, on Florence's twenty-first birthday, she gave birth to a girl. At the time she still believed she was married to Joseph. Then a letter arrived addressed to her husband. Florence opened it and discovered it came from a single woman called Marie Condie of 145 West Fourth Street, New York. Florence wrote back telling Marie she was writing to a married man. Maria replied that she had no idea Joseph was married as he'd told her he was a single man and had left Syria because he didn't want to go through with the marriage his father had arranged. The two women then found out that Joseph was lying. He had gone through with the arranged marriage and had a child with his wife. They were living with his parents in Syria. When Florence tackled him about it, Joseph did not deny it, so she said she would leave him and take her daughter with her. Joseph told Florence he would see her in hell first and punched her in her left breast knocking her over. The injury he caused gave her cancer and Florence had to have her breast removed. Once she had recovered she took her daughter and boarded a ship to England, but Joseph followed her.

Florence went to Retford, but Joseph wouldn't leave her alone and in early 1896 he pointed a revolver at her and the child and told Florence she had ten minutes to decide whether to give up the child or they would both die. To save the baby's life Florence handed the girl over and fled to Lincoln, hoping that at some future date she could get the girl back. Florence continued by telling them that she would sooner follow the child to the grave than allow her to go to Syria because if that happed the grandmother would sell the little girl to the Turks for £200.

Florence had only been resident in Lincoln a short while when she met an old friend from her childhood, Joseph Benson. On 29 March 1896, Florence gave birth to another child, Robert, and on 11 July 1896 she married Joseph in the Primitive Methodist Chapel in Portland Place, Lincoln. Florence and Joseph began writing to the father asking for her daughter to be returned but received no answer.

On hearing Florence's story the Guardians agreed to leave the child with the Jacksons and Florence went back to Lincoln for a couple of years before moving to Gainsborough and eventually to Scunthorpe. During that time she and Joseph had four more sons: Gerald (b.1900), Harold (b.1904), Clarence (b.1906) and Cyril (b.1907). In 1911, they moved to Horncastle. Florence died in 1951 in Brigg and Joseph died two years later.

Florence Spilman was born on 28 January 1876 to Robert Benson and Mary Ann Spilman (née Topham) in Alkborough. She was the oldest of seven children, John (b.1879), Jessie (b.1882), Sarah (b.1883), Anna (b.1886), Lucy (b.1888) and Henry (b.1890).

Described by the newspapers as a fashionable wedding, Florence Spilman married Joseph Pearson Walton (b.1856), the former chemist at the Frodingham Iron and Steel Company, on 8 October 1896. Lunch was at the bride's house and there was a dance in the evening after which the couple travelled by train to Lincoln and then onto London and Paris. They had two sons, John Spilman Walton (1900 – 1958) and Robert Noel Pearson Walton (1904 – 1989). In 1901 the family were living in Durham where they stayed for several years.

Joseph died on 28 March 1928 in Port Talbot and left £3,359.5s 6d to his sons who were both metallurgical chemists.

On 8 January 1898, Harry Driffield aged 6, of Raven Street, Scunthorpe, climbed the slag heap behind the Church Sunday School in Station Road with several other boys. The heap collapsed and although it was initially thought that none of the children were injured, Harry died of internal injuries the following day. Three months earlier his parents had lost their infant daughter after she was scalded to death.

The annual hiring fair at Scunthorpe took place on 17 May 1898 and was well attended. Wages for good cooks ranged from £16 – £18, housemaids £10 – £14 and general servants £8 – £10. Men's wages were: waggoners £16 – £18 (although one was hired for £26), second horsemen £12 – £16, boys £9 – £11.

Emma Dixon (née Elston) was born in 1849 in Barton Lincolnshire to Jane Elston. She had an older sister Jane (b.1846) and they lived with her grandfather John Elston.

Emma married Henry (known as Harry) Dixon in 1868 and had eight children with him: George (b.1871), Jane (b.1878), Ancel

Potato picking Ashby.

(b.1879), Ethel (b.1882), Harold (b.1884), Ada (b.1886), Edith (b.1888) and Oliver (b.1890). Harry was an innkeeper. The family lived in Chapel Street, first at number 67 then number 15. Harry died on 21 February 1898 and left £89.7s.10d in his will.

After his death Emma continued to run the Talbot Inn, but in order to sell beer she had to keep renewing the licence every six days. On 7 September 1898, she applied for a full licence at the Scunthorpe Licensing Sessions. This was granted and she continued to run the Talbot Inn. Emma died on 6 April 1926 aged 78. At the time she was living at 90 Mary Street, Scunthorpe. She left £1,181.15s in her will.

Louisa Unwin (née Hayes) was born in 1873 to Charles and Jane Hayes (née Morris) in Attercliffe, Yorkshire. She had two younger sisters, Charlotte (b.1877) and Elizabeth (b.1882) and two younger brothers, Charles (b.1880) and Tom (b.1888).

Louisa met Thomas Unwin in Yorkshire and they married in Sheffield in 1895. By 1901, the family had moved to Scunthorpe and were living at 19 Percival Street.

The following letter was from Private (8368) Thomas Unwin, a Reservist in No.6 company, 2nd Coldstream Guards who was fighting in South Africa. Thomas was a steel smelter at Frodingham and during his absence the steel smelters supported his wife,

Louisa and his three children, Charles (b.1896), Gladys (b.1898) and Bertha (b.1899).

The letter is dated 12 December 1899, written from De Aar and addressed to Mr. A Thurston, Manley Street, Scunthorpe.

> *We went through the battles of Belmont, and Graspan alright. When we took their position at Belmont they let us advance to within 80 yards of them and we could see no signs of life, but the next moment the whole world seemed to tremble and it fairly staggered us, but only for a second when we took their position by bayonet. The Scots Guards were the worst sufferers as they had the steepest positions to take. David St. John of the Grenadiers, and a Welshman too, was first upon their trenches, but got his head blown off after killing about four of them. One of the Boers fired at him with the muzzle of his rifle close to his head.*
>
> *Graspan we took without much trouble and then we came to the Modder River Battle, which I had not been in as I had been on outpost duty. The scouts managed to capture 25 of the enemy, who were looting cattle. I went to Cape Town with them as guard.*
>
> *At Da Aar I have broke my journey as the train to Modder River has gone and the next is at 5am, so I'm having an hour on my own. We lost our CO at Modder River and ten men, two more since died. Kimberley might get relief tomorrow. If so I shall not be here for it is 100 miles from here and Cape Town is 1040 miles away.*

Thomas survived the war and was awarded the South African medal. On his return Thomas and Louisa had another child, Ruby May (b.1903). Louisa died in 1904 aged 31. Thomas and his children moved to 10 Carlton Street where he died in 1958 aged 85.

Mary Ann Stanewell was born in East Butterwick in 1869 to William and Elizabeth Stanewell (née Hunter). William was a farmer and Mary was the youngest of four children. She had two older brothers, William (b.1857) and John Henry (b.1862) and two older sisters, Frances (b.1861) and Kate (b.1866). Mary married farmer Francis Newton (b.1866) in 1895.

Potato pickers Ashby.

On 26 June 1900, Francis Newton was in court charged with trying to murder Mary. They were at home on the previous Saturday and had had an argument. According to Mrs Bella Watson, who was in service with the Newtons, and in the house at the time, this apparently happened frequently. Mary went into the orchard to get away from Francis. Bella said she'd heard words between Mr and Mrs Newton and Mrs Newton went outside. She then heard Mr Newton ask for a gun. He took the one from the kitchen, but she didn't see him load it.

Mary was standing behind a tree when she heard a gun go off twice. Mary didn't feel anything after the first shot but after the second she felt something strike both her arms. She went into the house and saw marks on both arms and blood on the right arm and rushed off to her neighbour's house. Bella only remembered hearing the gun go off once then Mr Newton returned to the kitchen. The foreman, George Brumpton, was also in the house at the time. He took the gun off Mr Newton and locked it up.

Mary stayed with the neighbour, Mrs Harper, until seven o'clock then she and Mrs Harper took the train into Scunthorpe and saw Dr Beck. Mary stated at the trial that she was scared of her husband, but she knew he didn't mean to do it. Under cross examination Mary stated that her husband had never threatened her during their married life and that he hadn't done so on that occasion. When she returned from the doctors at about ten o'clock that night he'd apologised for what he'd done, saying he hadn't seen her in the orchard and had never meant to do her any harm.

Dr Beck said that although Mary was in pain, the wounds were superficial and not of a great depth and in his opinion were caused by spent shot fired from a distance.

Although bail was applied for it was refused as on 28 October 1899 Francis had shot at one of his Irish labourers, Pat Melbourn, whilst drunk after a dispute. He had been found guilty and bound over for £100 surety. He was given six months' imprisonment.

Mary filed a petition for divorce on 11 December 1900. The petition declared that contrary to her court testimony Francis had

Garden party turn of the century.

frequently threatened and assaulted her. She cited four accounts, May and December 1897, when he had knocked her down and kicked and struck her while she was on the ground. She also said he'd shot her in the hand on 7 May 1900, prior to the case which had resulted in him being prosecuted. Mary also stated that he had committed adultery with Ellen Marshall numerous times. However, the petition appears to have been cancelled and Francis was listed on the 1901 census with Mary. He died in 1917 aged 52. Mary died in Scunthorpe in 1964 aged 92.

CHAPTER TWO

1901 – 1914

Ada Sophia Swaby was born in 1874 in Lincoln to Robert Ingham and Elizabeth Swaby (née Sharpe). Robert was the manager of the Bluebell Hotel, Scunthorpe. Ada was the second youngest of seven children, William (b.1864), Arthur (b.1871), Walter (b.1873), Fancy (b.1867), Charlotte (b.1869) and Bertha (b.1878).

Pea Pulling team – turn of the century.

On 9 June 1903, Ada married William Robinson (b.1871 in Hibaldstowe), in Scunthorpe Parish Church. Ada and William lived at 38 Wells Street and William was an ironmonger. The couple had two sons, Arthur Roy born in 1910 and John Edward, born in the first quarter of 1911.

William died on 6 December 1940 and Ada died on 23 March 1943 leaving £5,971.2s.5d to Arthur and John who were ironmongers.

Margaret (Maggie) Laird was born in Coatbridge, Lanarkshire, Scotland in 1885 to James and Mary Laird (née Boyd). She had two older brothers, John (b.1873) and Abraham (b.1883) and two older sisters, Isabella (b.1877) and Mary (b.1879). She also had three younger brothers, James (b.1888), William (b.1890) and Joseph (b.1895) and a younger sister Jean (b.1892). James was an Iron Rolling Mill foreman. The family moved to Scunthorpe after Joseph was born and James started work at the steel works.

On Wednesday, 28 August 1903, there was a Ladies v Gentlemen cricket match in Scunthorpe. To make things more even the men were handicapped. While the ladies played in the usual way the men were only allowed to use their left hand to bat and bowl. Instead of using a normal cricket bat the men used an implement that was somewhere between a broomstick and a pick-shaft. According to the newspapers the ball was very slippery which made the game more amusing and Maggie Laird bowled very well. Unfortunately, the men won by four runs.

Maggie's youngest brother Guardsman (17833) Joseph Laird of the 5th Battalion Grenadier Guards died of wounds in hospital in England on 20 November 1916.

On 1 November 1905, Mary Benson of 39 High Street was found guilty of keeping a bawdy house and sentenced to two months' hard labour. Arising out of the same case a young married woman from Frodingham, Harriet Picksley, was found guilty of stealing a watch valued at 26s from Paul Hanbury of Scunthorpe on 28 October. She had been in custody since Saturday night and was bound over for twelve months under the First Offenders Act.

1906

Blanche Emily Howlett was born in the last quarter of 1882 in East Dulwich to Crosby and Eliza Howlett (née Simpson). Crosby was a plasterer. Blanche had an older sister Gertrude (b.1880), a younger brother Henry, known as Harry (b.1885) and two younger sisters, Eleanor (b.1888) and Dorothy (b.1891). Eliza died in 1894 and in 1896 Crosby married Maria Cliff in Caistor, Lincolnshire and they moved to Scunthorpe. By 1901, the couple had separated. Maria and her daughter Blanche were living at 108 Frodingham Road, Scunthorpe, Maria was head of the household and both women were dressmakers, working from home.

Scunthorpe Ladies Hockey Team 1903.

On 23 February 1906, 23-year-old Blanche Emily Howlett appeared in court accused of concealing the birth of her child by disposing of his body on 30 December 1905. On 2 January, some boys were playing on Glebe Pit in Scunthorpe when they found the body of a male child in a heap of soil, the baby was subsequently declared to have been born two or three days earlier. The jury was asked to decide whether Blanche knew she'd given birth and that the soil had come from the houses that ran along the back of the pit where Blanche lived with her family. Blanche had been engaged to a man called George and the marriage should have taken place the previous June, but the engagement had been broken off. At 3am on 30 December Blanche had given birth in the outhouse in the yard. Blanche said she had no idea she'd given birth. The jury found her guilty and sentenced her to two months' imprisonment in the second division.

Blanche married George William Hollingworth on 4 November 1906 and the couple had a daughter Dorothy in 1909 and another daughter Elizabeth in 1911. Crosby died in 1907.

Ivy Osbourne (née Watkinson) was born in 1906 in Lygon Street, Scunthorpe to Joseph and Betty Watkinson (née Pattrick). Joseph was a blast furnaceman who worked at the Redbourn Steelworks. Ivy had an older sister Annie (b.1904) and a younger sister Ena (b.1910). Ivy's earliest memory was of a funeral, known locally as a 'black'. First a cartload of peat was spread from one side of the road to the other outside the home where the person was dying and everyone spoke in whispers. The blinds were then drawn as a mark of respect in all houses along the street and remained closed until after the funeral. While the hearse and coaches lined up outside the house awaiting the mourners, the cemetery bell rang. The drivers and bearers wore tall black hats and the horse wore rosettes and was covered with fringed black cloths. Eventually a stout lady wearing a stiff black satin dress trimmed with black beads and a white frilled pinafore came out of the house. She handed a tray with glasses of wine and finger biscuits to the driver and then the coffin and flowers were placed in the hearse.

The mourners were all dressed in black with the ladies wearing black veils and the men black armbands. The other residents of the street stood some distance away to watch the procession pass and then they reopened their blinds. Eventually the mourners returned to ham, and seed cake and a borrowed tea urn from the chapel taking pride of place on the table.

Weddings were different at the beginning of the twentieth century too. After the guests had eaten the wedding breakfast someone would open the bedroom window and throw a plate of half pennies and wedding cake down to the children waiting in the street below. The plate had to be smashed during this process, although Ivy never found out why.

Ivy also remembered that further down the street there was a woman who owned a polished box called a promise box. This contained papers with writing on and every morning women came to the house and took out a piece of paper and read it out to the others. The message always seemed to be suitable for the recipient.

Ivy married Ernest Osbourne in 1927. She died in Scunthorpe in 1986.

Sarah Ann Fish (née Sanderson) was born in Greasbrough, Yorkshire in 1856 to Thomas and Ann Sanderson (née Butcher). Thomas was an agricultural labourer and Sarah was the oldest of six children. Sarah had three brothers, Hubert (b.1857), George (b.1862) and Alfred (b.1865) and two sisters, Harriet (b.1860) and Eva (b.1864). Thomas died in 1870.

On 16 August 1906, Sarah appeared at the Scunthorpe Petty Sessions accused of marrying Joseph Robinson, farm foreman of Warren Farm, Risby, while her first husband, William Henry Fish, was still alive. Sarah had married Joseph at the Brigg Registry office on 19 October 1905 having claimed she was a widow. Thomas Chawiss, who was half brother to William and had attended the first wedding in December 1887, said the couple had been parted about eight or nine years. He said William was alive and living in Frodingham where he had been ever since the marriage in 1887. Sarah was committed for trial in November with bail set at £40 from herself and £20 each from two other people as surety. Sarah appeared at the Lincoln Assizes on 23 November 1906 and was found guilty. She was sentenced to three months' hard labour.

Her daughter Lily Fish, aged 17, was also in court on the same day. Lily was born in 1890 and lived with her father William (b.1865), housekeeper Margaret Ellen Taylor (b.1865) and younger sisters May (b.1890), Annie (b.1898) and younger brother William (b.1893). Her youngest sister Edna was born in January 1901 although, according to Thomas Chawiss, Sarah had already left the family home by then. Lily was found guilty of trying to commit suicide on 13 November 1906. According to the prosecution Lily had been causing her father trouble and he refused to have her home so she had tried to hang herself. Lily was sentenced to six months' hard labour. She died in Gainsborough in December 1925.

1907

Although women could not vote in General Elections they were still involved in party politics. Lady Beatrice Prettyman spoke to women workers in Scunthorpe on 14 February 1907 in support of Sir Berkeley Sheffield, Unionist candidate in the forthcoming election. Sir Berkeley won the seat and entered Parliament on

The potted plant stall at St Lawrence' Parish Church garden party at the vicarage in 1907.

26 February 1907. He remained an MP until the General Election on 10 May 1929.

The Women's Co-operative Guild Scunthorpe Branch was inaugurated on 28 January 1908. Mrs Smith was elected secretary with Mrs Bradley president. Mrs Tock was elected vice-president and Mrs Walsham as treasurer. The committee consisted of Mrs Marshall, Mrs Waterhouse, Mrs Byles, Mrs Langton, Mrs Jackson, Mrs Knight and Mrs Stott.

There were sixty members and meetings were held weekly. In March 1907, they forwarded their first resolution to the Government: 'The Scunthorpe Branch of the Women's Co-operative guild earnestly asks you to bring pressure to bear on the Government to give facilities to Mr Stranger's Bill for the Parliamentary enfranchisement of women.'

This was sent to the MP for the constituency, Sir Berkeley Sheffield.

Kate Picksley was born in 1886 in Burlingham, Lincolnshire to Joseph and Mary Elizabeth Picksley (née Moreton). Joseph was a farm labourer. Kate had two older brothers, Edwin (b.1877) and George (b.1884) and two older sisters, Alice (b.1879) and Eva (b.1881). She also had two younger sisters, Eliza (b.1889) and Lucy (b.1890).

By the age of 15 Kate was working as a servant in the house of Thomas and Jane Spilman in Eastoft. Kate married Joseph Steels (b.1876) in 1903. Joseph worked in the blast furnaces and the family lived at 11 Mary Street, Scunthorpe. Their first child, George Edwin, was born in 1904 and their daughter Dorothy in 1905. Their second son, Joseph, was born in December 1906.

On Tuesday, 22 January 1907, Mr Philip A. Gamble held an inquest at Scunthorpe Police station into the death of a baby aged 6 weeks who was found dead in the bed of his mother. Kate had gone to bed at about 9 o'clock. Joseph and 3-year-old George slept in the same bed as his parents. Dorothy, aged 2, woke her mother at 8 o'clock on Monday morning because she wanted to kiss the baby. Kate then discovered that Joseph was dead and called a neighbour. Joseph was found lying on his left side and

Dr Balfour said the baby had died of suffocation. The verdict was that he had accidentally suffocated in bed.

The family moved to 12 Trent Street, Frodingham and had two more children, Nellie (b.1908) and Ethel (b.1910). Kate died in 1940, Joseph in 1954.

1909

On Wednesday, 2 April 1909, the Scunthorpe Lady Unionists Association held a meeting at the Public Hall in Scunthorpe. Miss Calthrop of the Women's Unionist and Tariff Reform Association gave an address on 'Our Colonial Empire and Tariff Reform'. Mrs H. Dickinson presided over the meeting which was well attended. Mrs R.E. Westwood proposed a vote of thanks to Miss Calthrop.

The following year, on 7 February 1910, Daisy Halling came to Scunthorpe. Daisy Halling was a well-known socialist, authoress and suffragette who had given up her career as an actress to campaign on behalf of women and the Independent Labour Party (ILP). She gave a lecture on The Elections and Religion in the ILP Hall on Monday evening and the meeting was very well attended.

1911

Elizabeth Hazeleay was born in 1857 in Sheffield. She married Henry Clipson from Barton in January 1907. In 1910, the couple moved to Scunthorpe from Barton and opened a second-hand clothes shop in Crosby Road, Scunthorpe.

On Friday, 5 January 1911, Elizabeth Clipson left the shop and went to Hull by train to do some business with a large sum of money. On the Friday night Elizabeth stayed with friends and the following afternoon she went to the pier in Hull to catch the 3pm boat to New Holland where she would catch the train back to Scunthorpe. It was due to arrive in the town at 4.30pm. The son of their mutual friend had gone with her to purchase the ticket and had seen the boat leave. Her husband Henry found a porter at New Holland who remembered carrying Elizabeth's dress basket from the boat and seeing her onto the train with her luggage. Elizabeth wasn't seen again. Her dress basket arrived in Scunthorpe but there was no sign of Elizabeth. At the time of her disappearance she had been wearing a sealskin jacket, a heliotrope hat and a brown costume.

Where Elizabeth disappeared to and why is a mystery, but Elizabeth had reappeared seemingly unharmed by April because she was on the 1911 Census. Henry died in June 1923 and Elizabeth in March 1927.

1912

Frances Martha Austin was born in 1912. She grew up on the Austin farm which had been in the family since 1850. When she was 13 she went into service in Devon. The place had been found for her by the local vicar and his wife who were family friends.

Frances met William Wright in Portsmouth and they married on 2 February 1943 and then moved back up to the area. They lived in temporary accommodation in Winterton to start with and Frances joined the ladies working at the NAAFI in Winterton. After the war the couple were housed in pre-fabs in Ashby. After her children had grown up Frances caught the bus to Grimsby every day to work in a biscuit factory.

Frances Martha Wright
(née Austin)

On 2 February 1912, Emily H. Watson (b. July 1882) became the new headmistress of the girls' department of the Scunthorpe Church of England School, later known as Gurnell Street School.

I, Emily H. Watson, assumed duties as Head Mistress of the Girls' Department. My appointment dates from February 1st, but owing to a misunderstanding which had arisen with the East Riding Education Committee about the date of my entering the services of the Lindsey Education Committee, I was called upon to make an explanation at the last moment. The rush and the anxiety which this necessitated to keep my appointment with the Lindsey Committee, bought about a violent headache. Hence I could not possibly travel to Crosby the same night on which my duties terminated at South Cave. Certificate number 19'65'94'354.

Emily's staff were all young women either boarding or living with their families locally and she records that attendance by the pupils was 88.5 per cent on her arrival.

Mary Constance Saxton was born on 26 May 1888 in Liverpool and christened on 17 June 1888 in Fairfield, near Liverpool. Mary was the daughter of William and Mary Saxton (née Owen). The family lived in Great Crosby in Lancashire. Mary had two older sisters, Elsie Violet (b.1880) and Hilda O. (b.1887) and three older brothers, William (b.1882), Ernest (b.1883) and Frederick (b.1885). She also had a younger sister, Evaline (b.1890) and a younger brother, Arthur (b.1892).

The year before she joined the Scunthorpe Church of England School, Mary was boarding at 94 Frodingham Road, Crosby, Scunthorpe with the Eaton family and teaching at the Elementary School for Girls as a County Council Teacher.

As the Second World War approached Mary was living at 125 Coppice Street, Oldham. She was still a schoolmistress. Mary never married and died in September 1944 in Crosby, Lancashire aged 56.

Lucy Rimmington was born on 21 October 1892 in Crosby, Scunthorpe to Frederick and Mary Rimmington (née Beacroft).

When she joined the Scunthorpe Church of England School she was living with her family at 91 Grosvenor Street, Crosby, Scunthorpe. Lucy was the oldest of eight children. She had three sisters, Harriet (b.1893), Flossie (b.1897) and May (b.1910) and five brothers, John (b.1895), Frederick (b.1906), Eric (b.1907), George (b.1909) and Vincent (b.1911).

Lucy was still a school teacher before the Second World War. She was unmarried and living at home with her parents and other siblings: Florence, Frederick, George, May and Vincent. Lucy died in Scunthorpe in 1967 aged 76.

Kate Muriel Butcher was born in Bures Hamlet in Essex in 1893 to Asa and Alice Butcher (née Goodson). She had a younger brother Reginald (b.1896) and younger sister Winifred (b.1897). While Kate was teaching at the school she was a boarder with Sarah and Charlotte Rowley at 1 Gurnell Street. Both Sarah and Charlotte were widows and earned their living by running a boarding house.

Alice Mary Whitehead was born on 20 October 1892 in Haxey, Lincolnshire to Albert and Alice Whitehead (née Parkinson). Albert was a general labourer. Alice was the oldest child and she had two younger brothers, Albert (b.1893) and Ralph Henry (b.1911) and five younger sisters Mabel (b.1894), Ruby (b.1896), Constance (b.1899), Norah (b.1902) and Edith (b.1905).

When Emily took over as headmistress Alice was also living as a boarder at 1 Gurnell Street. Alice married Robert Henry Tomlinson in January 1916. As the Second World War approached, Alice was living with her husband Robert at Station Road, Isle of Axholme. Robert was a farmer and they had several children. Alice died in 1960 in Poole, Dorset aged 69.

Lizzie Margaret Smith was born on 30 November 1893 in Liskeard, Cornwall to Charles and Marion Smith. Charles was a railway clerk. The family moved to 6 Clarke Street, Scunthorpe some time between 1901 and 1911 and Charles began working as a yard foreman. Lizzie was living at home when she started working at the school. Lizzie married William Walker in 1916 and during the Second World War they lived at 15 Cornwall Road, Scunthorpe and William was a crane driver at the steel works. Lizzie died in June 1975 aged 81.

Emily's first month as headmistress was quiet. Kate Butcher was ill on 3 February and there was a day's holiday for Shrove Tuesday. Attendance was good half way through the month, up to 89.1 per cent but by the end of the month was down slightly to 88.3 per cent.

School diary: March 1ˢᵗ. Miss L Wells commenced duties here this morning. The vacancy was for a teacher for Standards V, VI, VII but as Miss Wells has never had any experience with these standards and has only taught Infants since being certificated it has been necessary to change the teachers from the classes they are now teaching.

May 24ᵗʰ. The work for the past few weeks has dealt chiefly with the growth of the British Empire. Today, being Empire Day the girls in the Upper Standards represented the various Colonies, each girl carrying a tray with the productions of the Colony. In consequence of this the timetable was not adhered to this morning.

June 4ᵗʰ. Miss Elsie J. Mennell, Student Teacher. has been transferred from the Boys' Department into this Department. Miss Mennell will have Monday afternoons and alternate Wednesday and Friday afternoons, off duty at school.

Elsie Jane Mennell was born in Hull in 1893 and lived with her parents, Thomas and Phoebe Mennell (née White) and two younger sisters Phoebe and Maggie at 72 Frodingham Road, Scunthorpe. Thomas was a grocer's assistant. Elsie married Albert J. Everett in the summer of 1916. Albert was born on 8 October 1893. Their daughter Elsie Muriel was born on 20 July 1917. Albert survived the war and by the Second World War the family were living at 15 Doncaster Road. Albert was a soft furnishing draper and Elsie helped out in the shop. Their daughter, Elsie Muriel, was a teacher. Albert died in 1974.

School diary: 18ᵗʰ June. There is a holiday all day today on account of the trip to Cleethorpes.

19ᵗʰ June. The attendance this morning is very poor. Many of the children being too tired to get to school.

1ˢᵗ August Miss Edna Cutts commenced duties here today as a pupil teacher. End of school year.

Edna was born on 9 December 1895 and lived at 42 High Street with her parents John and Millicent Cutts and older brother Stanley. Edna does not seem to have liked teaching at the school very much and was absent several times during the next term.

School diary: Nov 15th. Miss Cutts has been absent since October. The Headmistress has had no word whatsoever concerning her absence.

By December, Edna had terminated her employment because of ill health. On 23 April 1927, at the Methodist Centenary Church in Scunthorpe, she married John Frederick Godfrey, the county dentist of Northamptonshire. She wore an ivory satin dress and georgette, a lightweight crepe fabric. The four bridsemaids were Miss Godfrey, sister of the bridegroom, and Hilary Binnington, Pauline and Cherry Coombe, nieces of the bride. Edna died in June 1988 aged 92 in Bodmin, Cornwall.

1914

In January 1914, Scunthorpe Urban Council was informed by the Medical Officer that the birth rate in the population of Scunthorpe was up 32.3 per cent, the death rate was up 18.2 per cent and infant mortality was up 20.2 per cent. The council agreed to appoint Nurse Huntsman at a cost of £30 per year as a part-time health visitor in attempt to reduce the high infant mortality rate.

Sylvia Florence Mary Brown was born on 9 March 1900 in Scunthorpe to Edward and Florence Minnie Brown (née Clayton). She was the oldest child and had three younger brothers, Edward (b.1902) John (b.1904) and Clifford (b.1907) and three younger sisters, Hilda (b.1903), Dorothy (b. 1905) and Freda (b.1914). Sylvia, known as Florence, also had another sister Ivy who had died at birth in 1911. Edward was a joiner and builder. When Florence was born the family lived at 104 Frodingham Road in Crosby and later moved to 1 Frodingham Road.

On Monday, 4 May 1914, 14-year-old Florence was fined 2s and 6d for failing to produce her licence while driving her motor cycle and sidecar in Scunthorpe. The police constable went to her home four days later and she showed him the licence then.

Florence married Alfred J. Walker in 1927 in Grimsby. She died in 1988.

On Sunday and Monday 21 and 22 June, crowds gathered outside the house of Hannah Smith and her husband in Crosby after the landlord tried to evict them. Eventually the rioting became so serious the chairman of the Scunthorpe magistrates, Mr J. Fletcher, read the Riot Act. Over 300 police had been drafted in from other areas to deal with the problem and after the reading of the Riot Act police immediately drew their batons and the streets were cleared. On Wednesday, 24 June Hannah appeared in court having accused the landlord, Thomas W. Pickthall of assault.

The court was told that the family owed 10s 6d rent. Hannah said that on 1 June she had paid the 10s and said she would find another house and then pay the balance. The landlord had agreed and given her a fortnight's notice. However, they had been unable to find another property and on Tuesday, 16 June Mr Tickthall, Mr Wass and another man appeared at the house. According to Hannah, the landlord said the family now owed him £1 3s, which she denied. The following day, the men gained entry by taking the coal house door off and after picking up a table and tipping all the crockery on the floor, breaking it, the men began removing the furniture. Hannah asked them not to take a certain picture. Mr Pickthall took her wrists and held her until the boy removed the picture. She struggled against him and he threw her in a corner against a wall. He took all the furniture except the bedding.

The landlord told a slightly different version. Mr Tickthall stated that Hannah had barricaded the front door, meaning the only way they could get in was via the coalhouse door. When breaking the door to gain entry the table had turned over breaking the crockery. Mr Tickthall claimed that he only grabbed Hannah's wrists because she had begun smashing up the furniture with a hammer and it was the only way he could get the tool away from her. Another witness, Joseph Pilsworthy, auctioneer's assistant, also stated that no assault had taken place despite Hannah Smith using filthy language. After a short period of deliberation the Bench decided that no assault had taken place and dismissed the case.

CHAPTER THREE

The Great War

School diary: 7ᵗʰ September 1914. Miss M Kirby commenced duties here this morning as an uncertificated teacher. She has had no experience whatsoever of teaching.

The girls are collecting to buy money for wool to knit socks and scarves for the soldiers. The upper girls are knitting socks, the younger girls are making handkerchiefs and scarves. The girls have bought a Tea Service as a wedding present for Miss Wells.

Mabel Carr was born in 1899 in Scunthorpe to George and Charlotte Carr (née Taylor). She had an older sister Edith (b.1895), older brother Robert (b.1896) and a younger sister Carrie (b.1909). George was a steam engine fitter and the family lived at 7 Francis Street.

Gladys Parker was born in 1900 in Goole to Richard and Alice Parker. Gladys was the oldest child and had two younger sisters, Constance (b.1903) and Alice (b.1910). Richard was a pawnshop manager in Goole and continued in this employment when the family moved to 56 Frodingham Road, Scunthorpe.

Mabel Carr and Gladys Parker held a Children's Garden Party in Scunthorpe on 18 September and raised £1 for the Belgian Relief Fund.

School diary: Oct 12ᵗʰ The girls have finished sufficient knitting and sewing to send the soldiers. 60 pairs of socks, 34 scarves, 23 belts, 33 helmets, cuffs 18 pairs, 25 pillows, 36 pillowslips, 3 pairs bedsocks, 60 handkerchiefs, 64 bedcovers, 2 sheets, 60 packets foot powder, 84 tins of Vaseline, 2000 cigarettes, 15 pencils, envelopes, notepaper,

60 pairs bootlaces. Invitations were sent to the parents of the girls and the gifts for the soldiers were displayed in the hall on Friday afternoon October 2nd.

Oct 30th The girls have been able to send this week parcels of knitting to the Crosby solders either on active service or going today. The parcels for active service contain more cigarettes and a scarf in addition to the normal supply. Every parcel contains 1 pair socks, 1 belt, 1 helmet, 1 mittens, 30 cigarettes, 2 foot powder, 1 pair boot laces, 1 piece of court plaster, 1 tablet soap, writing paper, envelopes, 1 small lead pencil.

Over the following weeks several lessons were abandoned as the girls continued to knit items for the soldiers.

The new president of the Women's Co-operative Guild was Mrs Paddison. She took over from Mrs King who had become president in 1909. Mrs Paddison remained president from October 1914 to October 1919. In November 1914, the Woman's Co-operative Guild held a meeting at which the speaker, Mrs Barton, discussed maternity. It was agreed that a resolution be sent to the Urban District Council: 'We are strongly of the opinion that a Maternity Centre is needed in Scunthorpe, and seeing that the Local Government Board are willing to pay half expenses, urge the Council to consider forming a centre.'

No action was taken by the council, so the resolution was sent in again. This time the council responded and the Child Welfare Centre was then formed. The sum of £2 was given by the guild to help to purchase scales to weigh babies.

On 11 November, the newspapers reported the death on 25 October of Private (5625) William Dann, of the 1st Battalion Lincolnshire Regiment. William was born in Broughton and had served in the Boer War. Before the war William had lived with his wife Susannah and child at 92 West Street Scunthorpe.

School diary: 18th December. The school is closed all day today. The girls are having a bazaar to raise money to pay for the wool used in knitting comforts for the soldiers and to buy more wool.

1915

In 1915, Mrs E. Williams, known as Daisy, was one of the first women to work at the steelworks. She recalls that on the first morning the girls didn't know what they would be doing so had no idea what to wear and one girl had arrived in a white pinafore which caused a fair amount of laughter. The women were put on various machines, turning, planing, drilling, shaping, slotting and driving overhead cranes. Although at first the men thought they would be useless, the girls soon settled down and did a very good job. Daisy completed five years in the gas blowing engine house at Frodingham Ironworks and for four and half years was a bye turn assistant engine driver. She was the first woman driver in the firm.

The women received their notice to leave seven months after the war finished.

School diary: Jan 22nd. The girls have been very busy this week preparing parcels for the wounded soldiers in the hospital at Boulogne. The parcels were sent off today. The sewing lessons in the Upper Standards are still devoted to knitting for the soldiers. During the drawing and painting lessons in Standard IV, the girls are painting postcards and selling them for money for wool.

Feb 1st. The Chairman of the Managers bought a soldier invalided home from France into school this afternoon. He thanked the girls for the knitted gifts sent to him while on active service.

Very many children are suffering from influenza and the attendance is exceptionally poor. 76 per cent

Over the next few months the school continued to provide comforts to the troops and when they weren't knitting the girls were raising money to buy wool.

The mid-May 1915 Hirings at Scunthorpe were poorly attended as by now many men had enlisted. Although there were young girls available for hire, experienced maids were very scarce. Wages for cooks in farmhouses ranged from £18 – £25 and cooks in gentlemens' houses £24 – £45. Wages for housemaids were

Scunthorpe and District Rifle club friendly match between teams led by Dr Berhendt and Mr Kiddle June 1915.

£16 – £30; General servants £10 – £25; parlour maids £20 – £30 and young girls £9 – £14.

Back at school, despite the war and the emphasis on knitting, attendances were still checked regularly and on the whole were very good. There were exceptions however.

> *School diary: Jul 10ᵗʰ. Eva D****, Standard III and Lily M*****, Standard IV have been playing truant this week. They have played truant several times before. Out of school no one seems to be able to keep the girls under control.*

As the school year drew to a close at the end of July more soldiers visited to thank the girls for their efforts and the staff shortage grew more acute.

> *School diary: Aug 31ˢᵗ. The girls have been presented with a piece of the bell of Salle Church, Belgium which was destroyed by the British to dislodge the enemy. The present was given by the 109 Field Company Royal Engineers.*

Matilda Coles was born in 1882 in Ludgershall, Buckinghamshire. She married Ernest Head in London in 1907 and the couple then moved to Brumby where Ernest was a policeman. After a few years, Ernest and Matilda moved to 21 Beauchamp Street and Ernest was working a slinger in the steelworks. In 1912 he left and became a carter at Frodingham Railway Station.

On 11 December 1915, Mrs Matilda Head received the news that her husband Lance Corporal (5823) Ernest Head of the 1st Battalion the Coldstream Guards was confirmed dead. He had been missing since 14 September 1914 in France. Because he was a reservist Ernest had been called up as soon as war was declared and after re-joining his regiment on 5 August he had been sent to France less than two weeks later. They had two sons Ernest (b.1908) and Stanley (b.1910).

The Group Scheme, often better known as the Derby Scheme, allowed men between 18 and 40 to either volunteer to enlist or attest with an obligation to come when called later on. In October the Government decided that voluntary enlistment would cease on 15 December. By the end of the weekend of 13 December 10,000 men had attested from Scunthorpe and the surrounding areas since the beginning of hostilities, 80 per cent of whom were married men. Nationally 215,000 men had enlisted and 2,185,000 attested, but 54 per cent of married men and 36 per cent of single men still hadn't registered so the attestation scheme was reopened on 10 January while the Government decided whether or not to introduce conscription.

1916

On Sunday, 3 January 1916, the Rev. J.H.C. Parker BA addressed a special service for men and women at Scunthorpe Parish Church on the subject of volunteers or conscripts. He compared volunteering in the army to volunteering for God's army and described those who hadn't yet volunteered or attested as either slackers, who found it comfortable and easy not to take their places in the army of the King of Kings, or those who did not join the Great Army because they hadn't given it any real thought. In his opinion the nation was going to its crucifixion so men needed to understand that they had to take the cross. He then talked about compulsion, explaining that there was no such thing as voluntary service because all service came from some compulsion, either from outside or from within. If the compulsion came from outside it was harder to accept than if it had come from within.

Maud Tinkler was born in East Halton, Lincolnshire in 1877 to William and Judith Tinkler. Her father was a bricklayer and Maud was the oldest of seven children. Walter (b.1879), Arthur (b.1881), Alice (b.1883), Edith (b.1885), William (b.1888), Ellen (b.1890). Maud married Alfred Turner in 1897 and they had five children. William Alfred (b.1899), Doris (b.1901), Alina Maud (b.1903), Edith Betsy (b.1905) and Walter (b.1908).

On the same day as the Rev. Parker was speaking in Scunthorpe Parish Church, Mrs Turner, now living in Frodingham, received some good news in the form of a letter from Lieutenant Hardy to say that her son William Alfred Turner of the 6th Lincolnshire Regiment was on a hospital ship suffering from frostbite. He had been reported wounded and missing since the first week in October. William Alfred was under age when he enlisted. He survived the war and in 1924 was working as a porter on the railways.

Girls from Frodingham school celebrating Empire Day during the First World War.

School diary: Feb 1ˢᵗ. During last night there was an air raid on the Steel works here. In consequence of this the children had very little rest so a holiday was given today. Two cases of diphtheria have been reported.

Three people were killed when the Imperial Naval Zeppelin, L13, captained by Kapitanleutnant Heinrich Mathy, flew over the town for eight and half minutes dropping twenty high explosive bombs and more than fifty incendiary bombs. The Zeppelin was overhead before anyone knew it was there and the first bomb was dropped in Ravensdale Street at 10.45 p.m. Four houses had the backs blown in and windows smashed. The houses next to them and those on the other side of the street also had their ceilings cracked, as did those in Mary Street and elsewhere. Large numbers of incendiary bombs were dropped in the Glebe pit and a high explosive bomb was dropped in Trafford Street which broke virtually all the windows. Another bomb dropped into the sewer on Wheatlands and an incendiary landed on Trent Cottages. The owner was Mrs Markham who was 86 and the widow of the founder of the Scunthorpe Co-operative Society. She threw a bucket of water on the incendiary and a neighbour threw it out of the window.

Another bomb was dropped near the foundry and two more in in the North Lincoln Yard, damaging the track and a railway truck. Thomas Danson and Jack Cyril Wright were killed when a bomb dropped in Redbourn Yard. The Zeppelin carried on and continued to drop incendiaries injuring four railwaymen and killing Wilkinson Benson of Ethel Terrace. Several people were blown over by the blasts, including a civilian who was blown through the police station doors. Superintendent Holmes was wounded and three windows were broken. People fled into the countryside in their night clothes.

The night Ravendale Street and Dawes Lane were bombed by Zeppelins Ivy Osbourne's baby sister was very ill with pneumonia. There was no penicillin in those days so mortality from infections was quite common. People were running towards Brumby Lane for safety and friends were knocking on their door trying to persuade them to leave the house. Ivy was terrified, but her older sister just shrugged and reminded her that everyone had to die sometime and Joseph, who was nursing the baby on his lap, refused to leave because he was sure his daughter would die if they took her outside. Ivy remembered that they eventually grew used to the raids and sometimes Ivy would go outside and watch when the airships were caught in the searchlights.

School diary: Feb 3rd. Miss Lucy Rimmington is suffering from Diphtheria. The girls are suffering from shock caused by the raid and it is impossible to work as usual.

Feb 7th The attendance is very poor indeed. Many families have left the town and gone into the country to live until the war is over. Many Welsh families have returned to Wales.

The threat of air raids continued, more families left for the countryside and several more cases of diphtheria were reported. Despite this the school continued its war work and the girls sent parcels of food to the prisoners of war in Germany. On 6 March only 36 per cent of children attended school after another air raid by Zeppelins overnight.

School diary: 20th Mar. Owing to the raid last night the attendance this morning is remarkably poor. And the children here are too sleepy for anything. There are only 115 girls at school making 41 per cent. Both teachers and scholars were so absolutely weary that everyone went home at eleven o'clock in order to get a little rest before afternoon school.

27th Mar. Miss Barley, the teacher of St 1, has been ordered to stay away from school for three months on account of a nervous breakdown. Many of the teachers are at present highly nervous. The alarms of the air raids and continual loss of sleep is proving very wearing. The fact that the school commences as usual the next morning prevents rest being taken.

April 3rd There was no school this morning owing to the air raids. There have been three successive air raids here, Friday, Saturday and Sunday nights and although no damage has been done to the town itself, aircraft visited places very near. The works were closed down and many people sought shelter in the country places. Many children have had no sleep whatsoever during the night, so have slept during the day.

Monday afternoon – the school reopened this afternoon with an attendance of 187 being 68 per cent. Many of the children are in too nervous a condition to work.

April 4th There was no school this morning, another air raid having taken place last night, Monday. Tuesday afternoon. The school reopened this afternoon with an attendance of 219, 79 per cent. Many children have gone into the country to live for this week.

April 6th. There was no school this morning owing to the air raid of last night.

Eva May Waltham was born on 24 June 1895 to Edmund William (1872 – 1939) and Annie Waltham (née Trimingham (1869 – 1957)) and baptised on 4 August at Goxhill, Lincoln. She had one sister, Norah Annie (b.1899). At the beginning of the twentieth century the family were living in Barrow on Humber and Edmund was a railway worker. The family remained in Barrow at Glencoe Villas, Barrow on Humber where Edmund was now a railway carriage and waggon maker.

By 1916, the family were living at 109 Digby Street extension, Crosby. Eva met Gunner George Kirk of Royal Garrison Artillery and the couple decided to get married. George was the son of Mrs A. Kirk of Goxhill. They were married on 12 May 1916 by special licence in the Wesleyan Church, the service being carried out by Superintendent Minister Rev. Daniel Heaton. Eva wore a dove grey outfit and navy hat. Norah was her bridesmaid and Gunner A. Kirk, brother of the bridegroom, was the best man. George survived the war and the couple had a son Raymond born in 1924. By the time of the Second World War the family were living at 42 Ferry Road. George was a railway carriage and wagon examiner while

Raymond was a clerk with a petrol supply company. Eva died in 1964 in Scunthorpe and left £2,282 to her husband and son.

School diary: May 3rd. There was no school this morning owing to an air raid last night.

May 12th. The sewing lessons in the Upper Standards have been given to the mending of socks and shirts for our prisoners of war in Germany. The girls are also refooting socks.

Staff shortages continued with teachers leaving to be closer to their homes or to undertake war work. Others were off sick and no replacements were sent. Supply teachers were now a normal part of the teaching staff.

*School diary: July 7th. Margaret P******, a girl in St I, played truant this afternoon. It has been ascertained that she accompanied a girl to Grimsby. Gladys J*****. has for a long time now exerted an evil influence on the younger girl. Many times she has caused trouble to St I teachers by standing on the railings outside the classroom and making remarks to the girls inside.*

Today has been very wet and the porch entrance is again flooded with water. All the winter time great inconvenience has been caused by the water coming through the ceiling. The Head Mistress has made many complaints but to no effect. Two windows have been smashed in Stage IV classroom during the evenings this week, evidently with stones. This is the second time the windows on that side of the school have been broken.

The girls continued to send parcels to France and to the prisoners of war and the school took part in the United School Demonstration held in aid of the Red Cross funds on 27 July.

School diary: Aug 1st. There was no school this morning owing to an air raid last night. The attendance this afternoon is very poor.

Aug 3rd. there was no school this morning in consequence of an air raid last night. These raids have a very disturbing effect upon the school work.

Edith May Rhoades was born in Kirton-in-Lindsey in 1896 to Thomas Sneddle and Annie Elizabeth Jane Rhoades. At the age of 4 Edith was living with her mother Annie Holmes, aged 22, and her grandmother. Her father, Thomas Rhoades, aged 40, was listed as a boarder. Edith had a younger sister Elsie who was born in 1900. Her mother died soon after.

At age 14 Edith was working as a general domestic servant to Arthur and Caroline Spilman. Arthur was a farmer.

Two years later, aged 16, Edith married George Herbert Tune (b.1893) on 9 October 1912 and her daughter Ida was born on 15 November 1913. Edith and George had another daughter, Elsie, who was stillborn in 1914. When war broke out George volunteered and joined the Lincolnshire Regiment. He went to France in September 1915 as Private 10935. He was promoted to corporal and wounded in 1916.

On 30 September 1916, Edith appeared in court, charged with trying to kill herself by taking laudanum. Her mother-in-law, Mary Jane Tune, pleaded for Edith to be bound over. She told the court that Edith had become like her own daughter even though she had twelve children of her own. Edith had married at 16, had a young child and hadn't seen her husband for over a year as he'd joined the army. He was now in hospital recovering from his wounds. She promised to look after Edith. After Mary's husband Antony also pleaded that she wasn't sent to prison the judge bound Edith over for twelve months.

George survived the war and they had another daughter, Frances, in 1917 but Edith died in December 1919. George remarried in 1920 and again in 1950. He died in 1973.

School diary: Oct 17th. The school reopened this morning with a fair attendance. Miss Mennell, the teacher of St I was married during the holidays. But owing to the fact of it being wartime and her husband a soldier, she will continue her work at the school just the same.

December 22nd. The Christmas holidays commence at noon today. The school will reopen on January 9th Tuesday. Owing to sickness amongst the teachers and the extra work it has been impossible to get the examinations for the quarter done. The anxiety for those in the war, the extra work, the cold rooms have made the teachers very tired during this term. The classrooms which face north have not once been comfortably heated this cold weather.

(The temperature on the 20th of the month was 48°F and so cold the children couldn't hold their pencils properly.)

CHAPTER FOUR

1917 – 1918

On 4 January 1917, Mary Frances Hannath, aged 67, married Richard Watson who was ten years older. Mary's cousin, William Hannath, gave her away and her niece, Jessie Burton, was the only

Station workers at Dragonby during First World War.

bridesmaid. Mary wore a grey costume with bonnet to match. Richard had lived in Scunthorpe for fifty years and had been married to Hannah, his first wife, for forty-eight years. Hannah had died 5 November 1914. Richard was a grocer and draper and had retired thirty years earlier through ill health.

School diary: February 16th 1917. The children have received two letters of thanks for the things they have sent to the French women and children.

The deaths of boyfriends and husbands in the war was sometimes too much. An inquest on the 20 February heard how the body of Beatrice Harrison, a domestic servant of Chapel Street, Scunthorpe, was pulled out of the River Trent, her coat, hat and other things found neatly folded on the bank. Her soldier boyfriend had been killed in action and several letters found at the scene suggest Beatrice was devastated by his death. The verdict was 'found drowned'.

Even in 1917 women had to deal with stalkers. On 4 April 1917, William Gibson appeared in court, charged with refusing to leave a grocer's shop in Ashby. The prosecution claimed Gibson had conducted a systematic persecution of the woman who owned the shop, sending her obscene postcards, making allegations about her and her house and chalking offensive statements on her wall. The court heard how the lady concerned was a respected widow trying to earn an honest living. Gibson had allegedly done the same thing to another woman the previous year. The defence considered him to be a dangerous man.

The Chairman of the Bench, however, decided not to hear the second charge. Instead he bound Gibson over, fined him £20, ordered him to leave Ashby immediately and to stop bothering women. Gibson was further ordered to find two people to provide surety for him, one for £10, the other for £20 and to pay £3.30s costs. Gibson paid his fine from the £20 in his wallet.

Emma Ellerton was born in 1861 and married Thomas Kirk on 22 September 1882 in St Mary's in Hull. The couple had fourteen children, Harriet Luisa (b.1881), Henry (b.1882), Fred (b.1887),

Ernest (b.1889), Harold (b.1892), Percy (b.1893), Lawrence (b.1894), Thomas (b.1895), George (b.1895), Annie (b.1897), James (b.1900), Dorothy (b.1903), Herbert (b.1905), including William Mills (b.1892), an adopted son.

In 1891 the family were living at 341 Trafford Street. Ten years later they had moved to 71 Trafford Street and Thomas was listed as a labourer. By 1911, Thomas was an ironstone miner and the family had moved to 60 Trafford Street.

On 10 May 1917, Emma was informed that her son, Private (240127) Percy Kirk of the 1st/5th Battalion Lincolnshire Regiment had died of wounds. Percy had landed in France on Good Friday 1916. He had just completed five years with the Lincolnshire Regiment (TA) and was attached to the transport section. On his way to the trenches Percy had his horse shot from under him. He received a gunshot wound to right leg and six gunshot wounds to his back and shoulder. Unfortunately, the gunshot wound to his leg had caused such damage that he had to have his leg amputated. The operation couldn't save his life and he died aged 23.

Four of Emma's sons, as well as her son-in-law and adopted son William, were fighting in the war. William had been killed and now Percy had too. Her other sons, Private (9863) George Kirk of the 6th Battalion Lincolnshire Regiment had been wounded in the Dardanelles on 1 September 1915, but survived and was currently in France. Lance Corporal Ernest Kirk had been in France since the beginning of war. He had been wounded twice, once in the head and the second time in the right hand and Corporal Harold Kirk was currently in hospital having been gassed.

Emma died in 1947 in Scunthorpe.

As staff shortages continued, Emily Watson, the headmistress of the Scunthorpe Church of England school, was ill for long periods and by 11 May Miss Rimmington was off school with a nervous breakdown. However, drill lessons continued, as did the patching and mending of clothes to send to the troops. Absenteeism increased and on 18 June Emily called in the Attendance Officer to investigate.

School diary: Jul 4ᵗʰ. There was a rumour in the town this morning that
enemy aeroplanes were making for this district. One mother came for
her girls, the mistress sent to the Post Office to ascertain whether there
was any truth with the statement. Being told there was none informed
the mother. Many children were kept at home in the afternoon.

Marion D. Bell was born in Glasgow in 1896 to John and Jane Bell
(née Logan). Marion was the oldest of six children and had three
brothers and two sisters, George (b.1898), Jane (b.1903), Elizabeth
(b.1905), Archibald (b.1907) and William (b.1910).

Marion married William Henry Morgan (b.1894), a steel worker
from the Frodingham Works, on 22 July 1916 and their daughter
Freda was born in August 1917. On 6 September, William was
arrested on a charge of assaulting his wife and persistent cruelty.
Marion applied for a separation order. She had applied for one the
previous November for cruelty, but the couple had reunited so the
order was rescinded. Marion also wanted custody of her daughter.
The case was remanded for a few days to allow William to sort
out his defence and his wife to arrange for legal representation.
William paid £20 for his bail.

The couple reconciled and in 1923 the family arrived in New
York. They moved to Indiana and had a son, Henry Junior Morgan
in 1927. They remained in Hammond, Indiana where William died
in 1983 and Marion in 1986.

Annie Briggs was born in Ashby in 1878 to George and Elizabeth
Briggs. She married Alfred Enefer (b.1876), a labourer, in 1897.
At the beginning of the twentieth century the couple and their son
George (b.1898) were living with Annie's parents. They had four
more children, Alfred (b.1899), Jessie (b.1901), William (b.1906)
and Minnie (b.1909). Ten years later the family were living at
11 Cemetery Road with Annie's widowed mother and Alfred was a
labourer at the Frodingham furnace.

On 12 September 1917, Annie took Alfred to court for persistent
cruelty to his wife and three children. A separation order was
applied for after the defendant admitted striking his wife. Alfred,
now a steel worker, maintained he was only the lodger. The first

separation order was rescinded and Alfred was ordered to pay 30s per week to his wife who was given custody of the children. He was also ordered to pay costs.

> *School diary: Oct 4th. There is a real indifference on the part of certain families towards the attendance of the children. When the girls are able to help with the housework they are kept at home very often. And when they come to school they have no interest in their lessons. This irregular attendance which is absolutely unnecessary has a disturbing influence. Some of the girls leave to go to private schools so they can stay away when wanted.*

Harriet Veal was born in Broughton in 1874 to George and Emma Veal. George was a farm labourer and Harriet had three older sisters, Mary (b.1869), Alice (b.1871) and Ann (b.1872).

Harriet married John William Johnson and they had seven children, Clara (b.1893), George (b.1895), Albert (b.1898), Carrie (b.1900), Charley Frederick (b.1902), Alice (b.1904) and Ernest Arthur (b.1905). By the time of the Great War the family were living at 18 Chapel Street.

On 15 October, the Admiralty announced that HM minesweeping sloop *Begonia* was now considered lost with all hands. On board was Leading Seaman George William Johnson, eldest son of John and Harriet. As a boy George had worked at Frodingham, but he much preferred the sea so on 11 October 1910 he joined the Royal Navy. George had been a member of the crew of the *Prince of Wales* when they landed the Australians at Sulva Bay on 25 April 1915 for the Dardanelles campaign.

In 1917, George was 22 and engaged to be married to a young lady from Scunthorpe who had two brothers who were also sailors. Looking forward to an early leave, George had published the banns for the first time on 14 October. His brother, Albert Henry, was also in the Royal Navy. An able seaman on a super dreadnought, Albert had been in the navy for three years and six months and had fought at Jutland.

Florence Taylor was born in Scunthorpe in 1884 to John and Emma Taylor (née Thomas). John worked at the Frodingham works as a foreman. Florence had an older sister Mary (b.1878), an older brother John (b.1882), a younger sister Maud (b.1886) and younger brother William (b.1901).

On 4 September 1907, Florence married Alexander Hugh Allen at St John's Parish Church, Scunthorpe. The couple lived with Florence's parents at 30 Frodingham Road and later at Lindsey House. In 1909, Florence had a daughter Elsie.

Hugh worked at the South Kirby colliery and 'Hughie', as he was known, was also a gifted amateur entertainer, known as the whistling comedian. In early 1915 he joined the Army Service Corps. Private Hugh Alexander Allen went to France soon after and while at base depot joined the company concert party called the Black and Whites. He gave many concerts for wounded and blind soldiers. Hugh went into action on 29 October 1917 and was not heard of again. A few weeks before his death he had transferred to the Artists' Rifles, part of the London Regiment. Florence was now a widow with two little girls. Hugh's younger brother Oswald, who had fought with the Canadians, had been killed in 1916.

On Saturday, 10 November, the teams of lady ammunition workers from Scunthorpe and Gainsborough played a football match at the Gainsborough ground to raise money for patriotic items. The ladies wore orthodox football attire and the ground had the largest attendance of the season. The first half ended 0-0 but in the second half the Gainsborough captain, centre forward Miss Williams, scored three goals. Miss Thorpe also scored, beating the Scunthorpe team 4-0.

Voluntary rationing had been introduced on 1 February 1917, the aim being to reduce the consumption of food that was in short supply and to avoid waste when cooking. Bread, meat and sugar were rationed. The weekly allowance for bread was 4lbs, the meat allowance (including bacon, ham, sausages, game, rabbits, poultry and tinned meat) was 2½lbs and for sugar the ration was ¾lb.

The scheme had some effect, but it wasn't really enough so a food control office was set up in the Harris Museum in Preston. This fixed the price of milk and butter from October 1917. However, shortages continued and while the more wealthy could afford food, malnutrition was seen across poorer communities. Standing in queues was time-consuming so mothers would often keep their daughters off school to do the shopping instead.

> School diary: Dec 7*th* Many of the girls stay at home to attend to the house in order that the mothers can go shopping or they themselves stand waiting to be served.

Harriet E. Parker was born at the end of 1897 to Arthur Raymond and Clara Parker (née Dixon). She had an older brother Raymond (b.1896) and a younger sister Alice (b.1903). The family lived at 117 Fotherington Street and Arthur was an iron moulder. Harriet had rheumatic fever as a child and when she recovered she became a member of the Frodingham Girl's Bible Class and also played the organ. She was a regular member of Frodingham Parish Church. The family moved to 53 Manley Street a few years later and then to the Old Brewery Manley Street. When Harriet was 16 she began working at G.L. Clayton's Millinery Department.

On 3 December 1917, Harriet died aged 20. Six weeks earlier she had seen a Hull specialist, Dr Eve, who'd told her to rest for a month. Harriet had done this and seemed better, but then she had a relapse. There were thirty-three floral tributes at her funeral.

1918

The problem of girls remaining at home to do the shopping continued in 1918 and the school was also facing a shortage of paper.

> School diary: Jan 14*th*. Owing to the difficulties concerning the food problem for the next few weeks the classes will take in geography lessons – foodstuffs – and where obtained and how conveyed to our

Staff at Scunthorpe and Frodingham Station during the First World War.

island. How we depend on other countries and what we get from them which are necessary for the health of our nation. The lessons are taken in connection with the Scheme of Geography. Each teacher has a small plan of the lessons available to the class.

Jan 29*th*. Two Australian soldiers visited the school this afternoon. They saw some of the file work, heard them sing and saw the drill and dances. It was the first time they had seen an English school.

Feb 1*st*. Many girls are away ill but many girls regularly stay at home to assist with the housework. So many homes take in lodgers that the girls are obliged to work at home as well as at school. The stock [sewing materials and paper] has not yet come. It is impossible to repeat the syllabus for needlework.

March 4*th*. Sent Violet R***** home today on account of the very dirty condition of her head. The school have excluded her but no improvement has been made.

March 5*th*. There are a number of girls away this morning waiting in the stores to be served with food.

March 13th. There was no school this morning owing to the air raid the night previous.

By the 15th of the month the girls were having to bring in their own materials to the sewing class because of lack of school materials.

On 26 March 1918, Edna Cutts, who had left the Church of England School at the end of 1912, was a bridesmaid for her older sister, Chrystabel when she married Paul Coombe. Paul was a clerk for Mr R.A. Symes, solicitor, and was a director of Scunthorpe United Football Club. Crystabel had been a teacher at the Scunthorpe Higher Elementary School.

School diary: March 29th. The other schools closed at dinner time today so many of the girls stayed away here in order to do the shopping for the weekend before the goods were all sold out. The attendance is always low when other children are having holidays and this school is open.

April 17th. Many of the girls were absent today. A circus being in town and as the other schools have closed for the children to go to the circus many of the girls went from here.

Ann Gilliat was born on 11 May 1834 in Waddingham, Lincolnshire to Edward and Ann Gilliat (née Kirby). At 27 Ann was living with her father and children Mary (b.1855), Edward (b.1858) and James (b.1861). Ann married William Stephenson (b.1835 in Driffield Yorkshire) in 1862 in Lincoln and had six more children, William (b.1864), Elizabeth (b.1866), John (b.1868), Charles (b.1871), Jane (b.1875) and Ann (b.1878).

By the beginning of the twentieth century Ann, William, Elizabeth, John, Charles and Ann's grandson, Leonard (b.1900) had moved to Scunthorpe. William died in 1906 and four years later Ann was living at 10 Princess Street with Elizabeth, John and her granddaughter Maud (b.1905).

On 12 June 1918, Ann, known to all as 'Granny', was gathering sticks on the light railway at Dawes when she was knocked down by eight waggons containing ironstone. Ann was 84 years old. The newspapers paid tribute to Anne saying that she was known as one of the best field workers in the area. They also commented on how fit she was by reporting that only a few weeks earlier she had walked to Waddingham via Kirton to see a sick nephew. The following day she had walked back, a distance of over thirty miles.

School diary: June 28ᵗʰ Miss Amy Curran has heard this week that she has been accepted as a student in the College at Sheffield.

Amy Curren was born 7 August 1899 in Scunthorpe to John and Amy Curren (née Doran). John was a shunter at the Frodingham Iron and Steel Company. The family lived at 66 Trafford Street and Amy had a younger brother Stanley (b.1903) and a younger sister Sarah (b.1909). Also living with the family were Francis Curren, a nephew (b.1900) and Lilian Lyons, a niece (b.1905). Amy married D'Arcy Addy in 1925. Amy died in 1980 in Laughton Forest Home, Scotter and left £39,439.

School diary: July 11ᵗʰ. So many are away with the influenza and so many who are in school seem unable to give their whole attention to the work.

July 16ᵗʰ. The Attendance Officer brought a note from the Medical Officer of Health this morning saying that influenza must be treated as an infectious disease and all cases to be notified.

Nov 11ᵗʰ. Very many girls are too ill to take any interest in their lessons. This morning the message came that the Germans had agreed the Terms presented by the Allies and at 11.30 the Managers came into school and sent the pupils home for the rest of the day. Holiday in the afternoon.

Nov 12ᵗʰ. Owing to some many children being ill and the rapid spread of the influenza the schools are closed by Medical authority until November 25ᵗʰ, thus giving nearly a fortnight to free the children of the disease.

Peace celebrations 1919.

The influenza outbreak at the end of the Great War killed more people than the war. It infected over 500 million people worldwide and killed an estimated 20 to 50 million.

CHAPTER FIVE

The Inter-War Years

1919 – 1923

The First World War had increased the need for steel and Scunthorpe continued to expand. Frodingham and Brumby had now merged and they eventually joined with Ashby and amalgamated with Scunthorpe in 1919.

As men came back from war those women working in traditional male roles returned to their homes. These homes had changed little in the intervening years. One lady remembers her house in Ashby. It was a three up, three down with a tiny scullery and small bedrooms. There was no plumbed water so there wasn't a bathroom. Water came from an outside tap shared with other families. The toilet was a bucket closet with a wooden seat that was cleaned weekly in the yard. The bucket was collected at night by the council. Toilet paper was cut up strips of newspaper on a string. There was no electricity or gas, so cooking was done on a range in the kitchen and this also heated the house.

Dorothy Witting (née Douglas) was born on 10 November 1919 to David East and Ada Cobb Douglas (née Willis). She had five sisters and two brothers. When Dorothy was 16 she went into service in London; one of her sisters was already there, also in service. Dorothy returned to Scunthorpe when she was 21 and began working as a clippy on Silver Dawn buses. George Witting had come to Scunthorpe from King's Lynn to work at the steelworks. George spotted Dorothy on the bus and followed the bus on his motorbike so he could speak to her. The couple married on 21 December 1940 and began their married life in a flat above the tobacconist in the High Street. Their oldest child, John, was born there. The couple then moved to Davy Avenue when John was 3 and later swapped to 5 Holland Avenue. Dorothy had ten children of whom John was the eldest. The brother and sister born after John both died. John remembers his mother baking her own bread on the open range. His father's brother was killed during the war. He had bought a motor bike from George and was driving back to his RAF base at Scampton in the dark when he drove into the back of a car.

School diary: The Medical Officer has closed the schools until January 6th.

The girls and teachers struggled with influenza, diphtheria and cold classrooms through to the Easter holidays.

School diary: April 28th. The school reopened this morning with a fair attendance. Many girls leave to go to private schools. They only attend a few times and then they stay away altogether – leaving school before they are 14 years of age.

May 2nd. The three trained teachers are leaving at the end of the month. All are accepting Headships. [Miss Gladys Key, Miss R. Oakland, Miss Atkinson]

July 18th. The school closed dinnertime today in order that during the afternoon preparations may be made for peace celebrations.

July 25th. The school closes this afternoon for the Summer Holidays. It reopens Sept 1st. The extra week has been given owing to it being Peace Year.

The Headmistress, Emily Watson, terminates her engagement here today after 9 and a half years of happy work with the children and especially so with her staff.

Sept 1st The school was reopened this morning. Miss Bertha A. Bannister commenced duty as the Head Mistress. Miss Bannister received her training in Lincoln College and her experience in Owler

Lane Girls' School Sheffield and the Church of England Girls' School
Scunthorpe. The classes were rearranged for the forthcoming year in
the following order:
St VI & VII Miss Lucy Rimmington
St. V a Miss Taylor
St V b Miss E. Rimmington
St IV Miss Morely
St III Miss Speight
St II Miss Wilson
St 1 Miss White

Bertha Annie Bannister was born on 5 August 1883 in Scunthorpe
to Bamford and Annie Bannister (née Boyens). She had two older
twin sisters, Mary and Sarah (b.1881), two older brothers Joseph
(b.1878) and Francis (b.1879), three younger sisters, Hannah
(b.1885), Isabel (b.1890) and Blanche (b.1894) and a younger
brother John (b. 1888). Before the Great War, Bertha was living
at home with her family at 27 Well Street. Bertha married James
Howard in 1920 and died in 1982 aged 99.

> *School diary: Sept 11th, Two cases of scarlet fever were reported today.*
> *The County Medical Officer of Health was notified of the same.*
>   *Sept 15th, Miss Grace Evelyn Parkin and Miss Gladys Elizabeth*
> *Marchland commenced duty as pupil teachers in the school today.*

Colds, sickness, mumps, Belgian Itch and scarlet fever took their
toll of pupils and staff over the next few months with cookery and
laundry classes being cancelled.

One lady from Scunthorpe received a letter from her friend
who had married the German teacher at a school in the south of
England. The couple had gone back to Germany when war was
declared and had remained there. The friend wrote how bad
conditions were and that having survived the terrible war people
were now dying of malnutrition and other diseases because of the
scarcity of food. Despite the war having finished nearly a year
earlier there was still no meat, eggs or flour in the shops. There

was usually only black bread and margarine with a few ounces of bacon fat on Sundays. Butter, milk and eggs were only available on the black market and very expensive. Butter was 30s per lb, milk 3s 6d per pint and eggs 1s 6d. The only legal way to purchase milk and eggs was through the doctor who gave out certificates but that only happened for those who were dying. They had queued for hours to buy one herring. Clothes were also in short supply with material costing £5 a yard, an ounce of wool 10s and a reel of cotton 12s. She said she was dreading the winter as she'd just paid £25 for two tons of coal.

> *School diary: Nov 11th the children were assembled in the Hall this morning when the King's letter was read as a reminder that this day is the first anniversary of the Armistice. At the eleventh hour there were two minutes of perfect silence when all thoughts were concentrated on reverent remembrance of the Glorious Dead.*
>
> *Standards V, VI, and VII attended a lecture in the Rink Cinema this afternoon when Dr Jacob, Travelling Secretary to the National Society for Prevention of Consumption addressed them on Consumption and how it is to be fought.*
>
> *Dec 3rd. Florence and Edna Bowes, sisters, have been sent through the Clinic to a Sanatorium in the West of England. They were taken, along with other children of the district, by the school nurse. Both children suffer from chest or lung troubles.*

Both girls survived. Florence died in 2000 and Edna in 1998.

1920

This was the year that brought changes to the school.

> *School diary: In order to meet the requirements of the new Education Act the Lindsey Education Committee has decided to alter the school year, which has hitherto commenced on August 1st so that it will commence on April 1st. As this necessitates putting the work, this year of two exams into one term, a temporary timetable has been drawn up giving more time to Reading, English and Arithmetic.*

Mar 23rd. The entrance examination for the Central School was held in this school today. The papers were on Arithmetic and English composition. The children eligible being those between 11 and 12; and those between 12 – 13, the former in St V upwards, the latter St VI and upwards.

Mar 26th The school will be closed on Monday as the buildings are required for the Town Council election.

Mr Burkett, accompanied by Mr Taylor, Higher Elementary school, called in this afternoon with respect to the children eligible for the Central School. He expressed pleasure at the quality of work shown on the papers. Places were offered to twenty-five girls, subject to the consent of their parents.

Mar 31st. A team of girls visited Appelby School on Monday afternoon to play a game of Captain Ball. A return match is to be played on the Crosby School ground this afternoon.

May 3rd. The attendance dropped considerably this morning. Much sickness, chiefly measles, chicken pox and influenza reported.

In June 1920, Maggie Windsor, originally from Ireland, appeared in court accused of breaking her neighbour's window and causing £2 worth of damage. When Police Constable Horton spoke to her Maggie was alleged to have said: 'I mean to have a revolution in Fenton Street, if I have to send to Dublin for some Sinn Feiners.' This caused much laughter in court. Maggie continued by saying that her neighbour, Mrs Hickling, had dared her to break a window. Maggie had obliged and then told Mrs Hickling to find Police Constable Horton and tell him that she'd dared Maggie to break the window and that he would probably say he was surprised she hadn't broken all of them. This caused more laughter. Maggie was fined 10s and ordered to pay 20s damages and costs. Maggie replied 'Oh my God, that's awful. How many days if I don't pay?'

The judge replied: 'One month.'

Maggie apparently responded. 'All right I'll have three.'

School Diary: June 11th. By arrangement with Mr H Watson, the Proprietor of the Rink Picture Palace, the children were able to spend from 2 o'clock to 3 o'clock in reviewing the picture on Sir Ernest Shackleton's Expedition into the Antarctic Regions.

June 22nd. As there is a Garden Fete today, to raise funds for the building of a new hospital for the district, the school is closed for this afternoon.

June 23rd. The school is again closed this afternoon on account of the Garden Fete.

June 24th As there is a Reception for Soldiers this afternoon to which soldiers' children are invited, the attendance is low this afternoon.

On 22 September a mass meeting of women was held in Scunthorpe with Councillor Mrs Hornby JP presiding and Mrs Frank Hett of Brigg and Miss Ashdown of Scunthorpe, the main speakers. The following resolution was carried unanimously: 'That the meeting of townswomen held at Scunthorpe deplores the decision of the miners to call a disastrous coal strike, which will cause untold misery and suffering to men, women and children and grave disaster to all our industry just recovering from the war, and urges that every possible means may be taken to avert such a calamity.'

School diary: Oct 29th Miss Bannister ended her service as Head Mistress.

Nov 29th. Miss Chown commenced duties as Head Mistress this morning.

1921

The new year did not start well. By February 1921, 70 per cent of iron and steelworkers were out of work with only two out of twenty-one furnaces working. Office staff were also being laid off and shops were closing down.

School diary: Jun 6th 1921. Lincoln High School girls visited our games field this afternoon and played a demonstration game of net ball, previous to which they played a short game with the Clayfield Road girls and then with Crosby.

In July 1921, unemployment was still a serious problem in Scunthorpe with 6,283 men, 332 boys, 104 women and 22 girls registered at the Employment Exchange. The amount of benefits paid out for the four weeks ending 1 July was £19,271 15s 5d. It was argued that the relief money was not being given out fairly, so after a discussion it was agreed that if a man found six days' work or more he would be stopped six days' money or more, depending on the number of days worked, but that periods of employment fewer than six days should not be taken into account.

Emma Eliza May Hillerby was born in Swinton, Yorkshire in 1898, the oldest daughter of Harry and Mary Hillerby (née Hicks). Harry was a barman. May had an older brother, Claude (b.1895) and a younger sister, Lucilla (b.1900). The family moved to Sheffield when Harry was publican of his own establishment and from there to Frodingham Road, Scunthorpe.

May was a member of the Frodingham Church Choir, a mezzo soprano who also played in *The Mikado* in Scunthorpe Amateur Operatic Society. She was also a very good actress who was once invited to join the world famous D'Oyly Carte Opera Company.

On 9 August 1921, May married Herbert Milan (b.1869), a retired confectioner of Doncaster, at Scunthorpe Parish Church. Herbert was a Freemason and member of the Doncaster Lodge. Herbert had been married before to Elizabeth (née Swales) who had died in December 1917. He had two sons, Ernest Swales (b.1904) and Harman Stainforth (b.1905).

May wore a navy blue travelling costume and lemon velour hat. Vinnie Bowden from Scunthorpe and Winny Bowers from Doncaster were the bridesmaids. They drove to Folkestone for their honeymoon. The couple lived at Christchurch Road, Doncaster until Herbert died on 24 December 1922. Herbert's estate went to probate and the money he left, £17,017 14s 5d, went to his son Ernest.

May travelled to Genoa in February 1931 and to Australia in the 1950s. She died in Doncaster in 1978, aged 81.

School diary: Sep 5th. Mr Addinson, by permission of the Lindsey Committee, delivered a Temperance Lecture this afternoon to Stds IV, V, VI, VII.

Sep 20th. By permission of the Chairman of the Managers 162 girls went to The Rink to see pictures of Treasure Island performance at 3 o'clock.

Oct 5th. Registers were closed at 1.30 today and the school dismissed at 3.40 as the netball team has been asked by Miss Terry to go to Brigg and demonstrate for the council school which is about to commence training for netball. One of the new buses came to the school and conveyed 39 girls and 8 of the staff to Brigg. The whole outing was good for the girls and thoroughly appreciated. The girls paid their own fares.

Oct 7th. At 2 o'clock today all girls from this department are being taken to the games field. The programme is as follows:

St VII Netball
St 1 Is Mr Bear at Home?
St IV & V Rounders and Captain Ball
St II & III Blacks and whites
St VI & VII Captain Ball
Auld Lang Syne
The whole performance is being arranged by the prefects.

On 12 October 1921, Hannah Marshall summoned her husband John Charles Marshall of 27 Clay Lane, Brumby to court for persistent cruelty. The couple had married at Brigg Registry Office on 27 December 1919. Hannah had first applied for an order on 13 August but had then stayed another eight days after which time she left and went to Hull. John then advertised for a housekeeper, Hannah saw the advert and returned home so the maintenance order was revoked. But Hannah now claimed John's behaviour was so bad she had started the claim again.

Hannah explained that after the court had given her 25s a week maintenance John wrote, asking her to return. As soon as Hannah did so John applied for a revocation order and locked her in the house so she couldn't stop him. Once the order was revoked John threatened to murder her, threw water over her and taunted her with how clever he'd been. He kept telling her to go and threatening to murder her if she stayed. The previous Sunday John had thrown cold water over Hannah at 4.30 in the morning while she was in bed and then ordered her to cook his breakfast an hour later.

John denied threatening to kill Hannah but did admit to trying to buy a revolver so he could practise in the back yard as he thought that might frighten her a bit. The Chairman of the Bench decided there was not enough evidence to make an order that day.

School diary: Nov 7. With the Chairman's permission the school is closed today, there being no heat. Temperature in no room was above 40° at 8.45. The lowest was 33°.

Nov 28th. On Oct 17th at the Manager's meeting, my postage of 8s.11d plus petty cash of 9s.5d were passed. I have not yet been paid.

The heating problems continued until December.

Elizabeth Gleadle, stage name Liz Smith, was born in Scunthorpe on 11 December 1921. Two years later her mother died in childbirth and when her father remarried he cut her out of his life. Elizabeth started going to the cinema with her grandfather when she was four and by the age of nine was acting in local productions. When the war started she joined the WRNS and met her husband while stationed in India. The marriage failed and Elizabeth bought up her two children on her own in Essex. Her love of acting continued and eventually she got her acting break in Mike Leigh's *Bleak Moments* and then *Hard Labour*. Liz became a household name as Letitia Cropley in *The Vicar of Dibley* and then Nana in *The Royle Family*. Liz died on 24 December 2016 aged 95.

1922

On 18 January 1922, Sir Berkeley Sheffield opened a new wing for Women Unionists at the Scunthorpe Constitutional Club and afterwards addressed a meeting, largely attended by men.

Co operative Society bakers in Winterton Road 1924.

School diary: Jan 26th 1922. On Tuesday 24th inst when I reached the playground at 1.15 I found Rose Powell crying. She had fallen and hurt her wrist. I rendered first aid and sent her home with a big girl advising the mother to see the doctor. Thinking it was a sprain the doctor was not seen until Wednesday night. He says it is a bad break. The school is in no way responsible. It was a pure accident.

Feb 28th. School closed all day for Princess Mary's wedding.

July 3rd. Kathleen Mason and Dora Jennings have been awarded Lindsey Junior Scholarships. Linda Cowling and Catherine Clitheroe were placed on the B list and are eligible for free places should there be any vacancies in the secondary schools. [Kathleen, Dora and Catherine were subsequently accepted for Brigg High School.]

Winnie Kent has passed the Feathers Scholarship exam and commences at the P.T. Centre in September. She was the only candidate from this school.

Gwendoline Wakefield was born in 1922. Her earliest memory is of starting at Gurnell Street School. Gwen passed her scholarship and went to the Scunthorpe Modern School. When she left school at 14 she went to Quartons Fruit and Veg company where she worked in the office. When the war started Gwen was 17 and her job was given to a war widow so she went to work in the florist shop. Wartime flowers were in short supply so they mainly relied on flowers from people's gardens, which they bought in, and one nursery in Barton that still grew roses, chrysanthemums and other flowers. The florist also sold paper flowers and lots of greenery.

Gwen met Mike at a dance in 1942. Mike was in the Eighth Army and when he came home in 1945 they were married.

1923

School diary: Jan 23rd. Following the letter received from the correspondent the time of morning school was changed from 8.45 – 11.45 to 9-12. The new time was started today.

Feb 27th. We have this week bought a gramophone for the school. (The money was raised by a jumble sale). The instrument will be used particularly for an accompaniment to the country dances – also for musical appreciation in connection with singing lessons. We have records of actual songs of a blackbird, thrush and nightingale. These will be used in connection with nature lessons.

May 7th the cookery and laundry centre has now been closed until further notice – as an economical measure.

May 28th 11 girls have passed the Preliminary Scholarship exam held by Lindsey Education Committee. Enid Manger; Jeanne Peck; Nellie Langton; Kathleen Kemps; Agnes Wodd; Kathleen Willy; Madge Foreman; Edith Clarke; Doris Brundy; Florence Jackson; Marjorie Beascock.

June 4th. The above girls have gone to the Central School today for the entrance exam for Secondary Schools.

July 3rd. By permission of the managers 179 girls have gone this afternoon to the Rink to see 'Hunting Big Game in Africa'.

July 5th. Some of the ST VII girls acted scenes from 'As You Like It' this afternoon

July 19th. 13 girls have been accepted for the Central School.

Aug 2 The 3 Primitive churches had a combined trip today to Cleethorpes. 109 girls were absent.

In August 1923, Dorothy May Rowe aged 18, a flax gatherer, threw herself into a reservoir at the North Lincolnshire Works in an attempt to commit suicide after a row with her boyfriend about another girl. In court Superintendent Johnson said Dorothy had been knocked about by her 19-year-old boyfriend several times but kept going back to him. The boy had even thrown her out of the house at one in the morning. The Chairman said he wanted to give Dorothy a chance to redeem her character so she was to stay away from the man, not try to kill herself again and not run around at night and the case would be adjourned for six weeks to see how she got on. Her parents were bound over to ensure she reappeared in court in six weeks' time.

Dorothy failed to appear in court on 29 September, her mother appeared instead saying Dorothy's father was in Sheffield looking for work. At first Mrs Rowe said Dorothy had been well behaved in the past six weeks before tearfully admitting Dorothy had gone to London with a man in a car. She didn't know who he was because she didn't think it was her business to ask her daughter who she was seeing. She also admitted originally lying to the police by telling them Dorothy had gone to London to see her brother who was ill.

Dorothy eventually gave herself up to Scunthorpe police and was taken back to court. Here she told the Chairman where she had been staying in London but refused to name the man she'd gone with. The case was adjourned again while the Scunthorpe police checked with London, but the address proved to be false so when Dorothy came back to court in October she was remanded in custody and sent for trial.

On 20 October, Dorothy was placed on probation and put in the charge of St Swithin's Home, Lincoln until a suitable home could be found for her.

When the Church of England school re-opened in September, cookery classes were transferred to the Central School. As well as reading, English (literature and poetry reading), arithmetic, dancing and games the girls were also taught history, geography, nature study, needlework and singing.

CHAPTER SIX

1924 – 1926

1924

School diary: March 12th & 13th 1924. 64 girls have these two days sat in this school for the Junior County Scholarship examination. 36 girls of 11 years of age; 28 girls of 10 years of age. An outside supervisor was present at each session.

In March 1924, Florence Edith Clark (née Lupton b.1890) was charged with bigamy. Florence had first married Peter Padrick Ratnayaka (b.1887 in Senegal) in Grimsby in 1913. Not long after that Peter found employment at the Appelby extension works as a rigger. Florence and Peter moved to Scunthorpe and moved in with George William Clark at 18 Santon Terrace. George's wife, Lydia Walhouse Williams Clark (née Foster), was ill and Florence looked after her.

In November 1920, Peter was carrying a block weighing about 8lbs and pulling some chains up to a joist on the roof at the Appelby Extension works. When he was about 6ft from the roof the ladder broke. Peter fell 18ft onto some bricks and the block fell on his head. The foreman erector told the inquest that the ladder was only two weeks old and was perfectly adequate for the job. The coroner examined the ladder and said that in his opinion it was utterly unsuitable. A verdict of accidental death was returned with the jury adding a rider that the ladder was not suitable for the work.

Florence remained at 18 Santon Terrace to keep house and look after Lydia. She died at the end of 1920 and Florence married George on 9 May 1922. They lived together for a while and then Florence went to Hull where she met George Silver. She told him she was a widow and they married and lived together in Hull. Florence admitted the charge and said she had a business to dispose of. She was placed on bail at a cost of £25 and £25 worth of silver.

In 1922, the hiring fair took place in May as usual, but according to the newspapers the young men and women who attended had little desire to be hired. A few well known waggoners were hired for £35 – £40, second waggoners £25 – £28 and young lads from £15 – £18.

Servant shortages were especially acute for parlour maids and good cooks. Wages for young girls were £15 – £20, kitchen maids and house maids £18 – £24, house parlour maids £26 – £30, good cooks £35 – £45 and cooks general £30 – £40.

On 2 June, the Medical Officer of Health, Dr Percy Horsburgh, stated that the new blouse worn by women was not the best protection against pneumonia. The birth rate for Scunthorpe was 24.6 per cent in 1923 compared to 25.5 per cent in 1922 which was still higher than the national average for towns of a similar size and population. The death rate was 9.9 per cent compared with 9.7 per cent in 1922, which was high but still compared favourably with the national average.

The Council's Sanitary Inspector visited the Provisional Supplies Company in Manley Street on 28 June. The company was owned by Ada Elizabeth Dook and her husband, Henry William Dook. The inspector seized 831 jars containing 1,400lbs of jam and had them condemned by a magistrate. According to the prosecution, the jam was full of mouse and rat droppings, maggots, chippings from the ceiling and cobwebs and the premises were filthy. In his defence Henry stated that the jam was not going to be used for human consumption and was going to be thrown away, however, he also stated that if the top was scraped off and the rest re-boiled with fresh jam it would be all right. On 9 October the court fined them £20.

There was a serious accident at the declaration of the poll for the Brigg Division in Scunthorpe on 30 October 1924. About 5,000 people had assembled outside the Wesleyan schoolroom where a temporary platform had been erected. Lady Sheffield, Lady Arthur Grosvenor, Miss Sheffield, Mr and Mrs Quibell and Miss Quibell were standing on the platform when it suddenly collapsed. They all escaped without serious injury, but two ladies in the crowd, Mrs George Hollingsworth of Carlton Street and Miss Betts of Frodingham Road, were knocked down and injured. They were carried into the building, almost unconscious but later were sufficiently recovered to be able to go home. Of the 33,124 electors, 26,860 cast their vote, 3,659 more than the previous occasion.

School diary: Oct 13ᵗʰ As a result of the lecture on 'teeth' by Mr Birels 168 girls have bought brushes and paste through him, off a firm in Hull. The timetable was changed to allow an opportunity to the girls of hearing Miss Saunderson LRAM of London recite. She recited a scene from Romeo and Juliet and a selection of lyrical poems.

On 12 December at 11.30 p.m., Mrs Rose Ellen Mulroy of 32 Porter Street went into her washroom and discovered the body of her husband Patrick Mulroy hanging from a beam. She cut him down at once and with help carried him into the kitchen but he was dead. Patrick, aged 47, was a blast furnaceman at the Normanby Steel Works. According to his wife he was normally a cheerful man but had been complaining of stomach pains for the past three months although he hadn't consulted a doctor. He smoked a pipe and was said to have 'smoker's heart'.

School diary: 1924 Inspection Report on Religious knowledge. The results this year show a marked advance on those of the last inspection, the oral tests were answered readily and well in every group and the Christian teaching of the various narratives was well understood.

Scunthorpe laundry's first delivery vehicle in the 1920s. The firm started up in 1907 in Clayfield Road, later renamed Doncaster Road. Miss Austin is driving with Miss Bradley by her side.

1925

By 1925, the population of Scunthorpe had risen to over 31,000.

Kathleen Tomlinson was born in Leeds on 10 May 1905 to Alfred Bates and Mary Elizabeth Tomlinson (née Atkinson). She had two older sisters, Dorothy Emily (b.1900) and Marguerite (b.1902). Alfred was the Scunthorpe Liberal Club Steward.

On 14 January 1925, when Kathleen was 19, she was stabbed in Carlton Street. A man approached her in the dark and said good evening. When she didn't answer he grabbed her by the shoulders and swung her around before telling her he was going to kill her and stabbing a sharp instrument through her cloak and dress, making two 3-inch wounds on her left arm and chest. He then ran off. Kathleen was unable to give much of a description, saying only that he was taller than her, wearing an overcoat and trilby and clean shaven. Alfred told the newspapers that he was convinced the attacker had made a mistake in the dark, thinking she was someone else.

There were two further attacks on young girls, both aged 16, in the vicinity of Gilliat Street the following night and reports in the newspapers stated that mothers were beginning to worry about letting their daughters out. The police did arrest a man for the attack on one of the girls, but it isn't clear if he was ever prosecuted.

Kathleen became a music teacher and at the end of 1941 she married William Parfitt-Pearce.

On 23 March, Minnie Reed, a 42-year-old married woman from Davy Road, was found guilty of stealing pork from the butchers of Raymond Atkinson and a cake from the bakers of John Atkins, both of Home Street. She was ordered to pay 5s costs as the court recognised that she had been having a bad time and the mental strain may have affected her actions.

The following day Ethel Maud Hammond and her 8-year-old daughter from the Carlton Café, Manley Street were charged with theft of a stone jar of strawberry jam and a tin of herrings from the grocers' shop of Mr Thomas Mennell of Robert Street. (Thomas was the father of Elsie Jane, who taught in the Girls' Department of the Church of England School in 1913 and had married Albert Everett in 1916.) Ethel was fined 10s and her daughter was bound over on probation for 12 months.

In April, unemployment rose again as another of the steel works, Normanby Park Steel Works, gave fourteen days' notice to over a thousand employees. The Redbourne Iron and Steel Works had already closed down the previous September and there were now 1,400 men registered at the Labour Exchange. Other than a brief spell of six months, all the steel works in Scunthorpe had been struggling since 1921. Because there were no other major industries in the town Scunthorpe had stagnated over the past four years.

There was a big attendance at the May hiring fair in 1925, but whereas there was plenty of work for second hands who were paid about £49, there was little work for waggoners at £58. Many of these more qualified men took the lower paid jobs. Wages for cooks were £30 – £40, parlour maids £28 – £40, general servants £26 – £30, housemaids £25 – £35, nursemaids and young girls £12 – £24.

In June 1925, a new maternity home in Scunthorpe was opened by Mrs W.J. Brooks. The house had primarily been designed to help

Opening of Scunthorpe Maternity Home 1936.

the poorest women in the town who were living in overcrowded conditions. In 1924, over 300 births had occurred in houses where more than four people were sleeping in the same room. These cases would receive priority as would those which were likely to be more difficult births. The charge was two guineas per week but if the patient was unable to pay then some or all of the cost could be covered by the rates. Payment could also be made by instalments.

Mrs Brooks said how wonderful it was to have such a home in Scunthorpe and marvelled at the great advances that had been made in the past twenty-five years. She thanked the County Council and Urban District Council for their work in promoting the health and wellbeing of residents. She also stated that anything started well in Scunthorpe always proved to be a success and she was sure that now they had secured such a wonderful home the people would support it and ensure it was the success it deserved to be.

Mr A.E. Dowse, Chairman of the Health Committee of the Urban District Council said the two councils concerned had collaborated in the establishment of the home which would do much to help the women of Scunthorpe. He urged them to continue their collaboration and build the long overdue Isolation Hospital at Brumby.

For the other women in Scunthorpe life continued. Women were still appearing in court, but the charges now included motoring offences. On 30 July, Alice Blair of De Tuyl Street was fined 20s for driving a motorcycle and sidecar dangerously in the High Street.

Betty Eastwood was born in June 1925. She was the youngest of six and remembers having a very happy childhood. Betty left school at 15 and went to work as a telephonist for Rose Brothers at Gainsborough. She remained there until 1957 when she was 32 and married Ronald.

Phillis Mary Middlemiss was born on 25 March 1905 in Sculcoates, Yorkshire, the youngest daughter of Arthur and Eliza Middlemiss (née Wilcox) who married in 1900. Phillis had two older sisters, Gladys May (b.1897) and Eliza (b.1899). The family lived at 13 Estcourt Street, New Bridge Road, Hull when Phillis was a child and Arthur was a paper manufacturer. As Phillis grew up the family moved from Hull to Cole Street where Arthur continued to work as a wholesale stationer and paper merchant.

Phillis trained at the Scunthorpe PT Centre (Pupil Teacher Centre) and then found employment as a teacher at the Doncaster Council Boys' School.

On 27 August 1925, Phillis married Cyril Uriah Petch, younger son of Mrs Petch of Somerby, Normanby Road and the late George Petch. Mrs Petch had lived originally in Cemetery Road but in November 1923 she had bought the extensive property known as Somerby on the Normanby Road for £880. Cyril worked at the Normanby Steel Works.

The ceremony was delayed for fifteen minutes because the bride's car was caught up in the Hospital Carnival procession. Phillis wore a white silk marocain dress trimmed with silver leaves and lace wheels and carried a bouquet of white lilies. She had two bridesmaids, Norah Wilcox, a cousin and Joan Liddall, a cousin of the bridegroom. They both wore peach crepe de chine with ribbon caps. The best man was Cyril's brother John. The reception was at Phillis's house and afterwards the couple left for their honeymoon in Scarborough, the bride wearing a fawn and pink knitted frock coat with black hat.

Ethel Mary Hunt was born in 1888 in Scunthorpe to Thomas and Emma Hunt (née Whitaker). Ethel had four older sisters, Martha (b.1875), Florence (b.1887), Lucy (b.1889) and Hettie (b.1886) and two younger sisters, Nellie (b.1890) and Eva (b.1899). She also had a younger brother, Tom (b.1891). Her father died at the beginning of 1901 aged 49.

Ethel married John Robert Preston on 11 August 1905 and they lived in Winterton. The couple had three children. Clarence was born on 29 September 1906 followed by Clifford on 7 November 1908 and Elsie on 14 March 1911. John enlisted in the Bedfordshire Regiment on 26 October 1914 as Private 21036. He transferred into the Royal Garrison Artillery in June 1915 and was posted to the Royal Engineers as Sapper 509611 in June 1917. The couple's third son, Robert, was born on 6 September 1917. John was discharged on 14 January 1918, aged 31, with asthma. He was given 3s 2d per week war pension. The couple had two more children before John died in the second quarter of 1924. The following year, Ethel, who was now 38 years old, was living at 60 Ravensdale Street.

On 31 August 1925, Ethel died in Scunthorpe Hospital after being taken ill the previous day. On 2 September 1925, the inquest into her death was opened and adjourned until 22 September to allow the police to make more enquiries. Dr Walter Salisbury of Grimsby and Scunthorpe had attributed her death to blood poisoning and septic peritonitis as a result of an abortion.

Ethel had made a statement whilst on the operating table of Frodingham Cottage Hospital but because the police had not found any corroborating evidence to support the name of the woman she had supposedly named, the coroner refused to allow the name to be mentioned. Dr Walter Salisbury told the inquest that Mrs Preston had told him she'd visited the woman five times, but he didn't think there was any compulsion on him to communicate this name to the police. The coroner stated that there was considerable difference of opinion amongst medical men about abortion. The jury decided there was no evidence as to who had carried out the operation.

1926

On 14 January 1926, Kate Goodall had only been a widow for three months when she met James Goodall. Sadly, James was only interested in her money and when she'd spent the last of it, he packed a bag and said he was hoping to find another woman to support him. The Scunthorpe Bench ordered him to pay Kate 10s weekly.

> *School diary: Mar 3rd This morning the head teacher left school at 10 o'clock to attend the police court as witness against Mr Waddingham who was being prosecuted by the Society for the Prevention of Cruelty to Children, for cruelty to his child, Ruth, a scholar in this school.*

On 10 March 1926, the Scunthorpe's Women's section of the Labour movement protested against the medical inspection of unemployed women.

In March, the Government gave a loan of £650,000 to the Appelby Iron Company, Scunthorpe to enable them to extend the works and complete the new steelplate mills. The money was needed to finish works that had started several years ago.

At the beginning of May, Mr and Mrs Frank Bunyan of 15 Porter Street received a letter from their son. This would not be remarkable except that Private Francis James Bunyan had been reported killed in action on 21 April 1918 (the first day of the German Spring Offensive when heavy casualties were incurred) and every year his parents put a memorial notice in the local newspaper. The letter was headed Gunner Bunyan, Number 30 Camp, Lark Hill, Wiltshire and had the most recent notice attached. Francis said that he was writing to say he wasn't dead, but because he knew they thought he was dead he'd just left it at that. He mentioned two friends from Scunthorpe, one from Sutton Street and another, Fisher, from Roberts Street and one from Broughton, Graves, whose mother had a newsagents in Pinfold. He went on to say he would be home the following week and he hadn't wanted them to get a shock. The letter ended with him re-iterating that there was no need to write as he would soon be home.

Mrs Bunyan had been ill in bed for weeks so Mr Bunyan and his daughter broke the news carefully. Their main concern was that it might be a hoax. Mrs Bunyan got up, washed and dressed and hurried off to verify that Fisher did indeed live in Roberts Street. Mr Bunyan and his son went to Broughton and spoke to Mrs Graves who verified that her son did have a friend from Scunthorpe although she didn't know his name. The family then compared the writing on this letter with that of previous letters from Francis. Although the writing was similar and signed James like the others, the envelope had been addressed differently, to Mrs J. Bunyan not Mrs F.A. Bunyan. The capital 'P's and 'B's were also different. They wrote to the commanding officer at Lark Hill enquiring whether there really was a Francis James Bunyan in the camp and asked for a reply by telegram.

The commanding officer immediately set about trying to find Francis but there was no one of that name in the camp so he handed the letter over to Superintendent Jones of the Wiltshire Constabulary.

The Bunyan family were members of the Bethel Town Mission in Scunthorpe at the time and the Pastor was Mr Joseph Olivant. On 28 May, the pastor received a letter from the police asking could they please break the news to the family that the letter had been written by Driver (1064828) Horace Graves, 79th Field Battery RA of Lark Hill Camp, Salisbury Plain as a joke.

Infidelity and marriage breakdowns are not new. On 20 May, George Thrower found his wife in a hut on some allotments with John William Dolby. When George Thrower asked John Dolby what he was doing, the latter attacked him, blacked his eye and hit him several times. Dolby was fined 5s. Mrs Dolby then accused her husband of threatening her with murder when she questioned him about his behaviour with Mrs Thrower. Dolby was bound over for twelve months and ordered to pay his wife's legal fees.

On 4 June, Samuel Pearce, a steel worker from Wilson Street, was granted a divorce from his wife Mabel on grounds of her misconduct with Thomas Cartwright of West Street. The couple had married in 1906 and had three children. After difficulties in the marriage they had separated in April 1921. The judge granted the decree nisi with costs to Thomas Cartwright.

On the same day the Brigg Guardians decided to ask Lindsey Council to begin operating the Necessitous Feeding of School Children's Act in Scunthorpe as over £600 had been given in benefits recently and there was enough evidence to show that many people were on the borderline of starvation and unable to feed their children properly.

On 8 June, the newspapers reported on the death of the Dowager Lady St Oswald at Appelby Hall near Scunthorpe. She was the widow of the first Baron, who was the MP for North Lincolnshire from 1865 – 1885, Lord of the Treasury from 1874 – 1880, and was created Baron St Oswald of Nostell in the West Riding of Yorkshire in 1885. Her grandson had succeeded to the title in 1919.

School diary: June 10th This morning the Co-operative stores supplied this department with 4 gls of milk for children whose fathers are out of work. The supply will come daily.

Although things were tight there was some work available for women as can be seen from an advert that appeared for a kitchen maid on 11 August, for Frodingham Cottage Hospital. 'Previous experience needed, 18 years plus.'

School diary: July 16th Vera Richardson has gained a scholarship.

During the week leading up to 19 October, a house in West Street attracted large crowds when an angel was seen in the window. The figure was about a foot high with a dove in its hand. A woman had died in the house and it was after that the angel had appeared. On the 19th, the day of the funeral, a large crowd gathered outside the house and several people claimed to have seen the angel. Once the cortège left the house the angel disappeared and was seen no more.

School diary: Nov 15th Free meals were started today in this department, the staff taking turns to supervise.

CHAPTER SEVEN

1927 – 1930

1927

On 1 March 1927, the annual report of the Lincolnshire Needlework Guild was issued by Lady Sheffield. The Guild was divided into eleven districts, each with its own vice president, 130 deputies and 1,447 members. The report stated that although contributions for the year were a massive 3,736 and these had already been distributed to various hospitals, welfare centres and other institutions, the Guild had yet to meet the same number of items donated during the war years. Nevertheless, the quality was just as good.

> *School diary: Mar 16th. 71 girls took the scholarship exam today. Apr 14th. A games field is now available for the girls to play on. This was used for the first time by the girls on March 29th. For two years there has been no field, neither is the playground possible for games in school hours.*

On 1 May, a professional dancer from John Street, Rose Adelaide Buckley, aged just 23, died under anaesthetic whilst undergoing an operation at Hull Royal Infirmary. Rose had been suffering from bronchitis and heart trouble since 1925 and the previous November had started having problems with her nose and head. The operation was halfway through when Rose stopped breathing and despite efforts to resuscitate her, she died.

As in previous years the annual hiring fair took place in May, but very few people were offered employment. According to the newspapers, plenty of labourers were hired, but second and third horsemen were scarce and didn't seem that interested in finding employment on the land. There were plenty of day girls and general servants looking for work, but few cooks, housekeepers and cook generals. Wages had fallen considerably and for cooks and cook generals these now ranged from £28 – £45, house parlour maids £24 – £35, ordinary generals £18 – £28 and young girls £12 – £20.

Pastor Joseph Olivant, who had helped the Bunyans after the cruel hoax perpetrated on them by Horace Graves, had something to celebrate. On 8 June, Gladys Mary Olivant, his eldest daughter married Stanley Field of Berkeley Street Extension at the Scunthorpe Wesleyan Church.

Gladys had been born on 19 September 1901 in Yorkshire to Joseph and Agnes Olivant (née Hill) while Joseph was a city missionary. Gladys had two older brothers Joseph (b.1898), Walter (b.1899), younger brothers, Sidney (b.1904) and Ronald (b.1925) and younger sister Agnes (b.1906). The family moved to Manchester and then to Scunthorpe when Joseph became the pastor of the Bethel Town Mission.

Gladys had been employed as a shorthand typist at J. Brown and Co Scunthorpe Works for five and half years, as well as being an assistant organist and her father's helper at the Mission. Stanley was the eldest son of Mr and Mrs W.S. Field of Henderson Avenue and, like his father, was a joiner and undertaker. Gladys wore an ivory crepe de chine dress trimmed with pearls, and a veil. She had a wreath of orange blossoms and a bouquet of lilies. There were two bridesmaids and two pages, the bride's sister wore pale mauve and Gladys's friend, Annie Grindrod, wore pale blue. Both wore black picture hats and carried bouquets of mauve and white sweet peas. Younger brother Ronald Olivant wore tussore silk and Barbara Hilton was in ivory net and both carried baskets of pink and white carnations. The best man was Walter Olivant, another brother of the bride. The reception was held at Old Crosby and then the couple left for Bridlington for their honeymoon. Gladys died in Beverley in December 1985.

On 1 October, Mrs Ethel Wood of 7 Winterton Road was making tea when her son, Harry Martin Wood, who was 12 months old grabbed hold of the teapot scalding himself on the chest, left arm and abdomen. Although first aid was given Harry died on 4 October. A verdict of death by misadventure was given.

The Right Honourable Viscountess Astor MP opened a new secondary school in Scunthorpe on 15 October. The school had provision for 250 children but the new part, erected at a cost of £35,000, enabled the school to cater for 400. Lady Astor emphasised the importance of all children staying at school until they were 16 and impressing on them a sense of moral and spiritual values as it was those values that allowed people to change the world for the better. She also said that while education was a blessing, it could also be a menace when corrupt regimes used it to tell their citizens what to think, as in Russia. In her opinion Russia was trying to put the brotherhood of man on a material basis without a spiritual foundation.

On 24 October, Herbert Richard Richardson, an electrician and greengrocer from 50 Cottage Beck Road, was charged with indecently assaulting a 16-year-old girl who'd been employed as a clerk in his warehouse. Eventually the charge was reduced to common assault and he was fined £5 which was the maximum allowed and costs of 17s.

On 7 November, Alice Miller aged 49 was found lying under the table with a coat over her head and a tube leading from a gas bracket under the coat at 16 West Street where she had been acting as housekeeper to Stephen Henry Carr. The inquest recorded a verdict of suicide while temporarily insane.

In December there was finally some better news as the Frodingham Iron and Steel Works reopened after being closed since the coal stoppage began. Two of the four furnaces had been lit and the other two were expected to be fired up in the next couple of weeks. Other firms in the district were also expected to start up again soon. Over a thousand men signed off from the Labour

Exchange on 19 December. For the women of the town it looked like things were finally improving.

1928

School diary: Jan 24th. By permission of the managers, 200 girls went to see 'Ben Hur' at the Jubilee Hall this afternoon.

Mar 7th The Scholarship examination took place today. 84 girls sat.

Mar 12th Snow fell heavily yesterday and today. Attendance this morning was 62.8 per cent.

May 1st The netball team carried off the trophy for girls under 14 years of age. This is the third year in succession that this picture (Atalautas Rex) has been won. It therefore belongs to the school. The over-14 team was again successful in winning the Lardelli Shield – this again was for the third year in succession. The excellence of these teams is entirely due to the splendid work of Misses L. and T. Rimmington all the year round in playing with the girls after school hours, it being impossible to use the playground in school time.

The annual Scunthorpe hiring fair took place on 14 May but although there were plenty of lads looking for work, very few were hired. Experienced men were very scarce as were capable cooks and cook generals. According to the newspapers there were plenty of young girls looking for work, but they wanted positions with big wages and plenty of time off. Wages were similar to the previous year with cooks being offered £35 – £45, cook generals £30 – £45, house parlour maids £28 – £40, experienced general servants £20 – £30 and young girls £12 – £20.

It was still very difficult to obtain a divorce, so couples would often come to an arrangement. The man would pay a woman to go to a hotel with him and then pretend to commit adultery. The wife would employ a private enquiry agent to catch them and then give evidence in court. Often the hotel proprietor and a maid were also called as witnesses.

Doris Blanche Way was born on 21 March 1891 in Eastbourne, Sussex to William and Annie Way. She had an older sister Margaret (b.8 October 1890), younger sister Elsie (b.17 November 1893) and younger brother Richard (b.1895). William was a job master working for himself at a stable.

At age 20 Doris was a draper's assistant and living at 47 Chelsea Road, Southsea with her widowed mother and her sisters and brother. On 7 July 1917, Doris married Eric Arthur Voisey in St Bartholomew's Church in Portsea. Private (392702) Eric Voisey was in 608 Company Labour Corps and was posted in September 1917. In June 1918, Eric was discharged as unfit for military service.

On 26 June 1928, Doris Blanche Voisey (née Way) asked for a decree nisi against Eric, now a draper from Blenheim House, Messingham Road, Ashby, after his adultery with a single woman, Miss Glasby from Yarmouth. Evidence was given by a private enquiry agent and the landlord and a chambermaid from the Bull Hotel, Bourne. The decree was granted.

In 1939, Doris was living at 64 West Common Lane with her mother Annie Way and her two sisters Margaret and Elsie. She was a woman's outfitter. Doris didn't marry again and died in 1981 in Cheltenham, Gloucestershire.

On 8 August, Kathleen Mary Taylor applied for an affiliation order (a legal document granted to a single woman stating that the man is the father of the child in question) against a 19-year-old man, Geoffrey Sutton from Wragby. The judge granted the order and Geoffrey was ordered to pay 7s and 6d per week and £6 5s 10d costs.

School diary: Sep 16th Joyce Stokes has gained a scholarship.

Peggy Qualter was born in September 1928. Her father worked at the steel works and was killed in an accident when she was 20 days old. Peggy had an older sister and her mother brought the two girls up on her own until she remarried later.

Peggy worked in the cinema as an usherette when she left school. At 17 she joined the ATS but didn't like it very much so only remained in for three and a half years. She married George who was in the Parachute Regiment and had to wait three years for married quarters by which time she had three children.

George stayed in the army for another twenty years and Peggy remembers this time as the best years of her life.

On the 27 September, Johannah Holt and her husband Victor, a fitter from Lanely Street, were sent to prison for neglecting their six children. According to the newspaper report the children's heads were covered in sores and their clothes filthy. The kitchen and bedroom were in a disgusting state while one of the beds was described as a mess of dirt. The larder was caked in filth and the dirt in most of the rooms swept to a corner and left. Johannah maintained that the children had never gone to bed without being washed and that they had been bathed on Saturday and Sunday. Both were sentenced to six months' hard labour. As he left the dock Victor kissed Johannah goodbye.

On 16 October, Mrs Mary Lizzie Padley (née Riply) who was 34 and the wife of Fred Padley, aged 29, a blast furnaceman from 88 New Santon Terrace, was found in the front bedroom of her sister's house in 18 New Stanton Terrace, fully dressed and lying on her back on the bed with a deep wound to her throat. An open razor was lying nearby covered in blood. Fred told the inquest that they had only been married for sixteen months and they had been very happy. The verdict was of suicide while of unsound mind.

The Sheffield family only lived at Normanby Hall for five months of every year. The rest of their time was split between their properties in London and Scotland. However, even though they were not resident, the family still sent hampers of dirty washing back to Normanby by train. The laundry building was away from the main house so the family couldn't see the maids doing the washing, drying and ironing. On good days the washing was dried outside, but otherwise the laundry was hung on drying racks inside and a stove was lit to try and speed up the process.

In 1928, Mrs Williams was the housekeeper. Mrs Williams wasn't really married but it was considered a mark of respect to address her as Mrs. Mrs Annie Goodburn (née Campbell) was the second kitchen maid, Maggie Dent was the kennel maid, Elizabeth 'Lizzie' Aldridge was the char woman and Ethel Drury was head housemaid.

Isabel Tosh was born in Ulverston, Lancashire in 1876, the eldest child of Edmund and Sarah Tosh (née Logan). She had two younger brothers, Walter (b.1880) and Hugh (b.1885) and two younger sisters, Marion (b.1882) and Lilian (b.1883).

Isabel married Augustus Henry Craystone Johnston (b.1864) in 1899 and their son Geoffrey Augustus Graydon Johnston was born on 11 July 1908 and died, aged 86, in Gloucestershire in July 1994. Augustus was a doctor and the family lived at 89 Frodingham Road in Scunthorpe. Isabel was a prominent member of Scunthorpe Women's Unionist Association, treasurer of a local girl guides group and on the Executive of the Scunthorpe Music Festival.

Isabel died aged 52 on 7 October 1928.

On 6 November, Mrs Alice Arnfield (33) of Davey Avenue appeared in court with her 12-year-old daughter accused of stealing a pair of wellington boots from J. Frisby Ltd, boot dealers. Alice pleaded guilty through poverty and the charges were dropped against her daughter. Alice was bound over for two years for the sum of £2.

On 12 December, Diana Sheffield, only daughter of Sir Berkeley and Lady Sheffield of Normanby Hall, was married at All Saints Church, Ennismore Gardens, London to the Hon. Robert Digby, second son of the late Lord Digby. As the Dowager Lady Digby had recently died the ceremony was much quieter than it would have been. Diana wore a midnight blue coat with a shawl collar and deep cuffs of dark brown fox fur and a velour hat with a spray of pink carnations. The only attendant was Nell Ward wearing a black cloth coat trimmed with beige fox fur, and a black velour hat.

By the end of the year the number of men employed had increased and there were now more men employed in the steel works than there had been in ten years. However, the number of women and girls employed had decreased steadily. In November the number of people registered as unemployed was 390: 249 men, 24 boys, 77 women and 40 girls.

1929

Ida Sturman (née Whitehead) was born in 1929 and moved to Scunthorpe in 1939. She was one of six children. Ida worked at Littlewoods and met John Sturman, known as Jack, when she was 16. The couple married the following year when Ida was 17 and Jack 21. Jack eventually became the Mayor of Scunthorpe in 1966-67.

> *School diary: 7.1.29 The school was reopened this morning after the Christmas vacation as a Junior Girls' School with 370 on the roll. All the girls are under 9 years of age. This number (370) comprises the junior section of the Old Doncaster Rd and Crosby Girls' school, 222 being from Doncaster Road.*

Edith Sharpe was born on 25 July 1900 in Stratford, Essex to Albert Emmanuel and Ellen Jane Sharpe (née Norris). She had an older brother Albert William (b.1893) and older sister Mabel Frances (b.1896). On 22 October, the family went to South Africa where her two younger brothers, William Coneybear (b.1905) and John George (b.1908) were born.

The family returned to live at 96 Silverdale Road, Tunbridge Wells, Kent. Ellen had died in South Africa and Albert was now a widower. In 1915, Edith's brother Private (10919) Albert William Sharpe of the South Wales Borderers died in Gallipoli.

After the war, Edith returned to South Africa and married Joseph Bowers (b.1875) on 19 April 1920 at St Cyprian's Church, Durban, Natal. Not long after they were married Joseph died and in December 1920 Edith, now a widow, returned to England with her brothers William and Jack.

In 1921, Edith married again. This time to Thomas W. Summers. The marriage was later dissolved. On 29 October 1927, Edith married William Leary Stuffin at the Register Office, Glanford Brigg, Lincolnshire. At the time Edith was living at 42 Cottage Beck, Scunthorpe and William at the Old Station House, Frodingham.

On 9 September, Edith, who was now 29 and living at 26 Sheffield Street with William and his mother, went into town to do some shopping. On her return she told her mother she wanted to lie down on the bed for a short time. A little while later her mother heard a crash and two screams. She rushed upstairs and found her daughter bleeding from a wound on her left side.

William Leary Stiffin explained that he'd borrowed a gun so he could go rabbit shooting and left it propped up in a corner of the bedroom that he and his wife shared. He'd been sure that the gun could not be accidently knocked over. Beside the gun was a box with three cartridges in. There were now only two.

Constable Marwood, who had been called to the house, stated that he'd spoken to the young woman and Edith had repeatedly said that it had been an accident. She'd been messing about and had not thought the gun would go off. The policeman added that he had no idea how she'd shot herself, but he was sure the wound was self-inflicted.

The jury at the inquest decided they were satisfied Edith had deliberately killed herself and bought in a verdict of suicide while temporarily insane.

William died in 1967.

School diary: 10.9.29 The MOH along with an official from the Ministry of Health examined the girls this morning in connection with the prevailing epidemic of scarlet fever. They found three rather suspicious cases.

Mavis Dales (née Hornsby) was born in Old Brumby in September 1929 and can remember sleeping on her grandfather's farm. She attended Ashby school and her father had the first haulage company in Scunthorpe which used Shire horses. Her uncles had several pubs in Ashby.

Henry Richard Jackson, a steel roller, was sentenced to twelve months' hard labour on 5 October after being found guilty of stealing a velour coat from Joan Mary Crofts when she was attending a Girl Guides' conference in Scunthorpe in

November 1928. He was also found guilty of stealing a cash box containing £150 from Matilda Fletcher. Matilda had a fried fish business and used to give Jackson some occasional work. She kept the box in her bedroom and after Jackson had finished some work in the bedroom for her in June she noticed the box was missing. The money was traced by police to Lincoln and found in the possession of another woman and they recovered £105.

Jackson, aged 54, was leading a double life. During the week he lived with his wife and at the weekend he changed his clothes and went to Lincoln where he lived with another woman with whom he'd had a child, pretending to be a wealthy gentleman with shares in South African interests. Jackson played the part so well he had even given her money so their child could go to a good school. Although Jackson came from a good family in Frodingham he had a record of poaching and gaming and had served a six-week prison sentence. He hadn't worked for two years, instead living off what his wife earned, either by taking in lodgers or going out to work.

Jackson was also charged with three other offences of theft in Lincoln. He had already spent several weeks in custody and his sentence took account of this.

On 19 October, Alice Arnfield was sentenced to twenty-eight days' imprisonment for receiving a pair of blankets worth 6s 11d her 13-year-old daughter had stolen from Scunthorpe Market. The girl was sent to a girls' home in Lincoln until she reached the age of 16.

Evelyn Allison was born in Ashby on 23 March 1909 to William and Hannah Allison (née Borrill). She had five older siblings, Ena (b.1899), Elsie (b.1901), Charley (b.1904), Mary (b.1906) and Grace (b.1908) and the family lived at 82 Frodingham Road. William was a steel worker.

Evelyn married Frederick George Barber (b.1905) early in 1928 and their son, Frederick George Barber was born on 1 June 1928. The family lived at 260 Ashby Road.

Evelyn, Frederick and baby Frederick, who was in his pram, were walking along the road on 24 October when they were hit by a car. Frederick and his son were killed and Evelyn was dragged

100 yards under the car. The inquest was adjourned until Evelyn was well enough to attend.

At the inquest on 12 November, Evelyn, dressed in mourning, her left eye covered with a plaster and having difficulty walking said she couldn't remember anything after she had checked the road was clear and stepped off the footpath.

The car had been driven by Major M.S. Banks of Burringham Road Ashby, a Director and Secretary of the Scunthorpe Brick and Tile Co.

Police Sergeant Killick suggested that the whole of Major Banks's car was on the footpath and that he drove for 45 yards after knocking down the pedestrians. Inspector Bradshaw and Superintendent Hutchinson both said they thought Banks was under the influence of alcohol, but four doctors testified he was sober and capable of driving a car.

The major said the night was dark and it was raining. He'd pulled out to overtake a parked car and hadn't seen the family until he was a yard away and then he'd braked and felt an impact. He hadn't stopped immediately because he didn't want to turn the car over and make things worse.

The jury returned a verdict of death by misadventure and that father and son had met their deaths by the negligent driving of Major Banks, but that he was not criminally culpable. The coroner commented that although they had to accept the judgment of the doctors, in his opinion people who drove shouldn't drink anything at all.

The following January, Evelyn was awarded £1,700 in damages which would be held in trust and given to Evelyn when she came of age. Through a solicitor Evelyn asked for an advance of £250 to meet her medical expenses and to enable her to purchase a property where she could rear poultry. The judge was a little worried and warned that the money had to last her for the rest of her life. Mr William Allison, Evelyn's father said he and his wife had experience in rearing poultry and were sure it would be a success. The judge agreed to the application for an advance.

In 1950, Evelyn married James Smith. She died in 1980.

On 28 October 1929, one of Scunthorpe's most famous residents, Joan Plowright, was born to William and Daisy Plowright (née Burton). Joan attended Scunthorpe Grammar School. She first appeared on stage in Croydon in 1948 and then in London in 1954. She married Richard Gage in 1953 and they divorced in 1960 and in 1961 she married Lawrence Olivier. The couple had three children, Richard Kerr (b.1961), Tamsin Agnes Margaret (b.1963) and Julie-Kate (b.1966). Both daughters are actresses. Joan continued acting until 2014 when she retired. The Plowright Theatre is named after her.

Emma Doncaster was born in North Leverton in 1847 to George and Eliza Doncaster (née Simms). Emma had an older sister Eliza (b.1843) and older brother William (b.1845) and eight younger siblings, George (b.1849), Sally (b.1852), Charles (b.1853), Laura (b.1856) John (b.1858), Millicent (b.1860), Hannah (b.1863) and Thomas (b.1866).

Aged 14, Emma was a dairymaid on a farm owned by Thomas Ledger's house in Rampton. Emma married Henry Brigs in 1869 in North Leverton and the couple moved to Scunthorpe where they had several children, Charles (b.1870), George (b.1873), Alice (b.1876), Emma (1878), Ellen (b.1880), William (b.1882) and Herbert (b.1885.) Henry worked for the Frodingham Works until the slump in 1921.

In November 1929, Emma and Henry, both 82 now, of 20 Ferry Road, Crosby celebrated their diamond wedding anniversary. Emma told the newspapers that when the first passenger-carrying flight had come to Scunthorpe several years earlier she and Henry had gone up and Emma wished she could have done the same to celebrate their anniversary. Only three children were still living, Charles, Alice and Ellen but they had twenty-two grandchildren and fifteen great grandchildren.

Henry died in the summer of 1933 and Emma at the beginning of 1934.

On 6 December, the seventy-two-bed Scunthorpe War Memorial Hospital was opened by Mr Talbot Cliff of Scawby in front of over 4,000 people. The town had hoped that HRH the Prince of Wales

Staff at Scunthorpe Memorial Hospital 1930s.

would be able to open the hospital but had received a reply in September from his private secretary that the Prince's diary was sadly full up until Christmas. He was intending to visit the area soon though.

CHAPTER EIGHT

1930 – 1933

1930

By the 1930s many houses had not improved much since the previous decade. One lady remembers as a child that the kitchen had a range with a side oven. The fire was kept burning all the time and most food was cooked on the open fire. She remembers that breakfast was always a cooked meal and that when she started work she would come home for her midday meal. The main meal was always eaten at lunchtime – soup, stew, pies, rice pudding – and tea was bread and butter, sometimes with jam, although she remembers her parents occasionally having fish and chips for supper.

School diary: 9.4.30. 157 girls were each supplied with 1/3 pint of milk at a cost of 1d this morning. The milk is to be supplied daily.

On 15 April, the school won first prize for school string orchestras at the Scunthorpe Musical Festival.

School diary: 15.5.30. Report by Mr J. Maudsley HMJ School Inspected 24ᵗʰ Jan 1930. About fifteen months have elapsed since this department became for juniors only, in accordance with the scheme of reorganisation in the district. Owing to the pressure on the accommodation in the contributory schools it has not yet been found possible to organise this department for children up to eleven years of age. The children who were last promoted to the Senior Department

ranged from 9 years and ten months to 10 years and ten months and no
child who will be promoted in September will be 11 years old.

June Robinson was born in June 1930 at 2 Lindum Street Ashby. She went to Henderson Avenue School and remembers having scarlet fever as a child and spending ten weeks in the isolation hospital.

When the war broke out June was living in Crosby Avenue and she remembers the German bombers flying over on the way to bomb Hull. She could tell they were German planes by the noise of the engines and she recalled that they would stand at the bottom of the garden and watch Hull burning. June hated the Anderson shelter and tried not to go in if she could help it. She remembers not wanting to get out of bed when the air raid siren went in the night and because her brother would be crying her mother often didn't take them outside. Instead they would get under the dining room table. Her father was very cross when he found out and he would make them go outside and into the shelter. June can't remember ever being frightened but her younger brother who was only two and a half was scared. Her father worked at the steelworks on shift work. The shifts were very long but he still found time to join the Home Guard. She remembers him bringing home a Sten gun which they weren't allowed to touch.

When a bomb dropped in Buckingham Road behind them and cracked the ceilings, her mother papered over them. Several years later June was in bed when the bedroom ceiling began to fall down. It didn't come down in one piece because it had been papered. A few years later the downstairs ceiling also fell down.

June left school at 14 and got a job in the Co-op fashion department where she was paid 18s a week. She met her husband at his twenty-first birthday party in St Paul's Church Hall when she was 16 and when she was 19 they married. She was then earning £3 11s a week, but as was the custom, she had to give up work.

1931

The country was now into the second year of the Great Depression which had started in October 1929 and, although there were lighter moments, life for the women of Scunthorpe became harder.

A postcard sent by Mrs W. Compton of 21 Elsie Street, Goole to her sister, Miss M. Woolsey of 72 West Street in 1906 finally arrived on 5 January 1931. The postcard bore a green halfpenny stamp and the Goole cancellation mark and was believed to have gone astray in Scunthorpe.

There was still some work for women available. On 23 January, an advert in the *Lincolnshire Echo* sought a companion in Scunthorpe, aged about 36 for a good home with a small remuneration for companionship. Other adverts called for cooks, general servants, maids and housekeepers.

Mrs S. Blackburn of Crowle, near Scunthorpe won 5s in the *Sheffield Independent*'s 'Cooking dos and don'ts' on 27 February for her recipe for a quick and simple supper meal which used up left-over vegetables. 'Place boiled cauliflower on the bottom of a greased pie dish then grate cheese over it, add one thinly sliced tomato and salt and pepper, then add more cauliflower and so on until the dish is full. Put potatoes on top and some butter and cook

War Memorial hospital 1930s.

in the oven. For a quick sweet, make a custard with three eggs and a pint of milk, open a tin of apricots and place in a glass dish then cover with the custard and serve hot or cold.'

Annie Newstead, aged 20, of Lloyds Avenue was awarded £47 2s 6d on 21 February for injuries she sustained whilst riding pillion on her boyfriend's motorcycle the previous August. Frank Stephenson, a plumber, was driving back from Blackpool to Scunthorpe when the bike was hit by a Rolls Royce driven by Henry Carden of Manchester. Annie sustained a fractured ankle.

Phoebe Campion was born on 27 March 1892 in Lancashire to David and Mary Campion (née Howard). She had an older brother Charles (b.1883) and older sisters, Ellen (b.1885) and Jane (b.1889) and a younger sister, Bertha (b.1894) and younger brother, William (b.1897). David was an old iron dealer.

Phoebe met William Ainsworth during the war and they began living together. On 11 December 1915, Phoebe was listed as his wife on his attestation form for the Royal Garrison Artillery. Phoebe and William married in March 1916 and their son William was born in April 1916. William went to France in 1917 and then to Mesopotamia. Meanwhile Phoebe hadn't heard from him so she wrote to his regiment in February 1918 asking where he was as she was very worried. The regiment contacted Basra who explained that William had been hospitalised in March 1918 with influenza. He returned to duty and was hospitalised again in June 1918 after which time he had been struck off fighting strength whilst awaiting a decision as to his future. In 1923 William re-enlisted in the Territorial Army. According to his service records he joined 4th Battalion KOOR, however I have been unable to find this regiment, although I have found a mention of William in the Cheshire Regiment in 1923.

On 10 March 1931, Phoebe Rebecca Ainsworth, aged 38, of 49 Grosvenor Street appeared in court and pleaded guilty to claiming to telling fortunes three days earlier.

Mrs Day, wife of Police Constable Day, said she went to the Central Rooms Scunthorpe where Madam Mays, a clairvoyant and crystal gazer, had a canvas tent. Mrs Day waited her turn and when she entered the tent she handed the clairvoyant a crystal which Madam Mays covered with a black cloth and then placed in her left hand. Phoebe then asked if Mrs Day's husband was in work and when Mrs Day nodded she said he would soon get a rise. Phoebe added that her husband was a charming man and good looking too, a man anyone could be proud of, but she should be wary of a little fat man. Phoebe also said she could see a soldier who wanted to give her a message and that in May Mrs Day would receive a long box, but she shouldn't accept it. Mrs Day was also told she would be successful in two years' time, more so than she had been in the past five. Mrs Day asked how much she owed and Phoebe said it was up to her, so she gave the clairvoyant sixpence.

Mrs Marwood, the wife of another police officer, also visited Phoebe. She was told she had a good husband and that they would never want for money or food and her husband was going to be given a better position. Phoebe also told her that there was a spiritual message from an old lady but she couldn't quite see it and if Mrs Marwood would like to go to her house she would be able to tell her more and it would be very joyous news. Mrs Marwood gave Phoebe 2s 6d.

PC Marwood told the court that Phoebe had said she thought she was all right telling fortunes in the Central Rooms as the manager shared the money with her. Phoebe said she was very sorry as she hadn't realised it was illegal, but her husband had been out of work for thirty weeks and they needed the money. The court fined her 20s. Phoebe then asked if it was all right for her to read palms instead.

William died in December 1967 and Phoebe died in March 1970 in York.

Maud Priest was born in Scunthorpe in 1905 to Daniel and Ada Priest (née Walker). She had an older sister Florence (b.1892) an older brother Arthur (b. 1894) and a younger sister Lillian May (b.1910). Daniel was a steel worker.

In August 1927, when Maud was 25 and living in West Street, she met James William Watson. James told her he was from Middlesbrough and single. They married in Brigg in September

1927 and subsequently had three children Arthur (b.1928), James (b.1930) and Ada (b.1932).

On 13 March James was charged with bigamy. His wife, Edith Watson, from Hymer Street North Ormseby, Middlesbrough said they had been married in May 1920 and that they had three children. James had left her in May 1924 and although she had a maintenance order of 15s a week, he had only paid for two weeks.

James pleaded guilty on 10 September and the judge sentenced him to ten months' imprisonment.

At the end of March Mrs Harriet Tock and her husband had gone to bed in the High Street when she heard someone tampering with the window. She climbed out of bed, opened the blind and saw a man standing close up to the window. When her husband came over to the window the man stared at them for a moment and then ran away. Lawrence William Whittingham aged 28, a rigger from Cottage Beck, New Brumby was charged with being on enclosed premises for an unlawful purpose. He pleaded guilty to that charge and several others and was sentenced to nine months' imprisonment.

The unemployment figures for May did not make good reading. There were now 2,575 men over 21 unemployed, 263 18 – 20 year olds and 100 boys. There were 91 women unemployed, 170 girls and 83 18 – 20 year olds.

Carrie Carr, a school teacher from Francis Street, was killed on 20 May while riding her motorcycle on the main Lincoln to Brigg road. She turned sharply towards Kirton Lindsey near Redbourne and the machine skidded on the wet road throwing her off. Carrie was taken unconscious to a farm and then to the hospital but later died. She was 22 and had left college a year earlier to take up employment at Crosby Council School.

On Saturday, 21 May, Elsie Jones, second daughter of Alderman R. Jones, a farmer of Conesby, married Hugh Johnston, son of Dr Johnston of Scunthorpe at Frodingham Parish Church. Elsie wore a gown of parchment satin and had a long train of silk lace. She carried a sheaf of blue delphiniums. Her bridesmaids were her sister Ida Jones and her niece Joan Horwood. The honeymoon was taken in the south of England and the continent.

June Mrs Lucy Hall, from Marchbank, Bury, widow of John H. Hall of Bury, was appointed matron of the Scunthorpe and District War Memorial Hospital. The hospital had opened in December 1929 after the cottage hospital at the junction of Cliff Street and Rowland Road, built in 1886, failed to meet the requirements of the sanitary authority in 1892. Talk of a new hospital to cope with the expanding town began in 1914 and after the Great War ended it was decided to dedicate the new hospital to the memory of those who had died in the war. A committee was set up in 1925 and raised over £11,000. Lord St Oswald donated 14.5 acres of land and the foundation stone was laid in October 1927.

To add to the misery of the Depression there was an earthquake in the Hull and North Lincolnshire district on 7 June. The tremor lasted seventy seconds and did some damage, mainly near Hull. Virtually all Scunthorpe felt the tremor, one person describing it as a dull thud followed by a tremor that shook the bed and made pots and pans rattle. At the Trentside Works a cast iron roller belonging to the Southern Oil Company burst. In Doncaster Road there were fears that recent heavy rain had dislodged the hill behind their homes, but although some ceilings were cracked and bits fell down, there was little other damage. The last time Scunthorpe residents had felt an earthquake was when one occurred in Lancashire in the early 1900s, but one woman recalled that tremor had been shorter than this one.

Alice Roberts met Corporal Harry Fox of the Lincolnshire Regiment during the war when he was on leave from France and they married in March 1918. Their son Stanley was born in December 1918.

Harry had left Alice shortly after being demobbed in December 1919 and she hadn't seen him again until she'd been called to court in Swadlincote as a witness in November 1930. Harry, now 40 years old and working as an engine winder whilst living in Osgathorpe in Leicestershire, had married Hilda Bonser at Linton near Swadlincote on 2 April 1923. He was now on trial for bigamy. Whilst in court Alice gave Hilda a sympathetic hug. Harry was found guilty and the court bound him over for two years. In June

1931 Alice Fox was granted a decree nisi from her husband Harry Fox and custody of her child.

On 24 June the Scunthorpe lady golfers, known as Holme Hall Ladies, played the Market Rasen Ladies on the Warren Course in Market Rasen. The Market Rasen ladies won by six games to two. The Scunthorpe ladies who won were Mrs Stansfield who beat Miss Norledge and Mrs Rose who beat Mrs Abrahams.

Elsie May Ward was born in 1899 to Harry and Harriet Ward (née Limpson). She had an older brother Jack (b.1895) and older sister Gladys (b.1898), a younger brother James (b.1904) and three younger sisters Ethel (b.1901), Nellie (b.1908) and Amy (b.1910). Harry worked at the Frodingham works, first as a labourer and then in the blast furnace.

Elsie married Frank Mumby in September 1920 and their daughter Joyce was born the same year. Reginald was born in the summer of 1924 and Joan in June 1930.

On June 23 Mr Justice Acton granted Frank a decree nisi, against Elsie who was now living in a caravan in Scunthorpe with a Mr Butler.

On 16 July Scunthorpe held its seventh annual Hospital Carnival on the Co-operative Society employees' sports ground and over 30,000 people attended. There were over 170 entrants in the procession and Rhona Stephenson of Winterton, a pupil at Scunthorpe Secondary School, was crowned queen by Dodo Watts, the film star who had appeared in the 1925 film *Confessions* when a child and more recently the 1930 film *The Middle Watch*. She was accompanied by Donald Calthrop, producer, actor and film star of *Blackmail* (1929). Rhona, who was born in 1918, wore an old gold robe and was driven in a decorated coach drawn by two white horses.

Florence Eliza Kennington was born in Scawby, Brigg on 4 February 1863 to John and Ann Kennington (née Broughton). John was a painter and taxidermist. Florence had three older brothers, John (b.1854), Charles (b.1856) and George (b.1861) and an older sister Ann (b.1858). She also had two younger brothers, William (b.1865) and Ozias (b.1868).

In April 1881 Florence was 18 and a servant in the household of William and Mary Ann Robinson in Hull. She married George White in the last week of July of the same year and the couple lived in Brigg. They had seventeen children although six died at or just after birth. Surviving children were Jane (b.1883), Charles (b.1886), John (b.1887), Flora (b.1889), Albert (b.1890), Lily, (b.1892), Sydney (b.1893), Grace (b.1893), George (b.1896), General (b.1900) and Elizabeth Maria (b.1905).

In 1905 the family moved to 9 Home Street, Scunthorpe and George began working at the Frodingham Steel works as an iron fettler.

In the last week of July 1931, Mr and Mrs George White, now living at 50 Trafford Street, celebrated their golden wedding anniversary. Of their seventeen children, four sons and five daughters were still living. George had loved fishing and won over a hundred sweepstakes, five gold medals and come third in an all-England competition and fourth in a world competition. Two of their sons, Charles and Albert, had been Lincolnshire champion cyclists. Albert was the most famous, holding the record for English championships and winning more prizes than any other cyclist in the world. Between them Charles and Albert had won over £10,000 in prizes.

George died in June 1934 and Florence in March 1951.

In September there was more bad economic news for the town when news broke that the last blast furnace in operation at the Trent Works was due to be damped down with the loss of a hundred or more jobs. This was the third works to be closed down in the last two years. Only the Frodingham and Appelby Iron and Steel Works (United Steels Ltd) and the Normanby Park Iron and Steel Works were still operating.

Eileen Victoria Hamilton-Cox was born on 27 October 1891 to Colonel Arthur Francis Hamilton-Cox and Susan Josephine Hamilton-Cox (née van de Riet). She had an older sister Freda (b.1890), four younger brothers, Cecil (b.1893), Howard (b.1894), Arthur (b.1897) and Harry (b.1900) and a younger sister, Margaret (b.1904).

During the First World War her brothers, Second Lieutenant Cecil Francis Hamilton-Cox of the Duke of Wellington's (West Riding Regiment) and Captain Howard Jack Hamilton-Cox of the Royal Marine Artillery, were killed in action within three months of each other in 1917.

On 24 September 1931, Eileen was the private secretary to Lady Sheffield. She went riding with her groom and had been trying to take a sharp bend near the top road to Winteringham when the mare suddenly bolted and fell. The horse skidded for 28ft and Eileen received a fracture at the base of the skull and damage to her brain. She died in Scunthorpe Hospital that night. Eileen left £424 2s 10d to her mother Susan Josephine Hamilton-Cox.

News that the Redbourne works were to close at the end of November was not welcome. The population of Scunthorpe was now 35,000 and total unemployment in the town was already 2,108. This closure would add another 1,500 men to the register. In November 1928 unemployment stood at 482, this had risen to 626 in November 1929. Men were standing on street corners, hopelessness on their faces. The short hours and low wages had already left many in debt.

Emily Gomersall was born in Hull in 1895 to Martin and Ann Ellen Gomersal (née Barraclough). She had an older brother, Hubert (b.1893) and two younger sisters, Florrie (b.1897) and Phyllis (b.1901). Martin was a shoe and boot repairer with premises on Market Hill.

After leaving school Emma went to Scunthorpe with her parents and worked as a dressmaker before becoming a missionary. She had been the Sunday School teacher at the Frodingham Parish Church and her parents lived in Clarke Street.

After Emily had been accepted by the China Inland Mission she went to the Bethnal Green Hospital in London to learn nursing. From there she went to China in September 1926. Back in Scunthorpe Emily's sister Phyllis married the Rev. H. Whitcombe in 1927, at the time he was the curate of Frodingham Parish Church.

Having spent two years in Shanghai, Emily now moved to the Bordon Memorial Hospital, Hankow. On 11 October she wrote to her parents, stating the post was intermittent and they weren't getting any news and they had no idea what was happening elsewhere in China. She mentioned that two other lady missionaries had arrived recently who had been robbed but were otherwise unhurt. Her parents hadn't heard anything since but because Emily had joined the mission for seven years her parents were not expecting her home for another three years.

In December, newspapers were full of the story of two missing women missionaries in China. Mrs Hayward and Nurse Emily Gomersall were reported to have been in grave danger from bandits. At the time of their capture Mrs Hayward was very ill and Emily was about to take her to the coast for surgical treatment. Captain F.H.A. Staples, an officer with the Indian Army, had set out with a rescue party the previous day with M. Oberg, a Swedish missionary and Chinese officials hoping to escort the women to Pao-tou Chen in northern China. On the 8th, news reached Scunthorpe that Captain Staples had sent a telegram to Peking stating that the two women were safe in the Mengel Hill camp, 30 miles from Pao-tou Chen.

Meanwhile, two Irish missionary priests, Fathers P. Laffan of County Limerick and J. Lineham of County Cork, had been released after being in hands of bandits since April and had finally arrived at Hankow on board a gunboat. Both were in very poor health and suffering from dysentery and had been taken to hospital. Emily's parents breathed a sigh of relief, but it seemed the women weren't safe just yet. Later, a further message from the British United Press said the two women and their rescuers had been surrounded by bandits about 30 miles from Pao-tou Chen, Mongolia. Officials in Suiyuan had then sent telegraphic orders to the nearest troops to disperse the brigands.

By 8 December Emily was on her way by train to a hospital in Peking and telling her story to the newspapers. She had been taking Mrs Hayward to Peking when they were joined by a wealthy Chinese man carrying furs and gold who was accompanied by Mongol bodyguards. They were travelling on foot and were about 30 miles from Pao-tou Chen when they were attacked by bandits on horseback who took them hostage hoping to ransom them. There was a fierce battle between the bandits and the Mongol guards who were beaten back for a while. When they'd gone the bandits robbed the party and then the Mongols reappeared. They finally fought off the bandits and took the party into the mountains. There they had remained trapped for eight days in the bitter cold while the bandits surrounded them.

On 28 December, Scunthorpe Urban Council decided to ask Lindsey Education Authority to start providing free school meals to needy children in the district. The council considered that conditions were now worse than in the previous crisis in 1921.

1932

In February Scunthorpe Urban Council let it be known that they weren't happy with the Lindsey Education Authority's refusal to put the Feeding of Necessitous Schoolchildren Bill into effect despite several councillors offering to provide ample evidence of starving children in the town.

Views towards attempted suicide had gradually softened as can be seen in this case. Constance Coy was described in court on 15 February as a girl who had never had a chance. Constance's mother had died when she was 11 and Constance, now 18, was working at the Temperance Hotel in Holmes Street. On 1 February Constance went missing. Eventually the police had broken down her bedroom door and found her lying fully dressed on her bed. The gas bracket above the bed was on and Constance was barely breathing. The police were very concerned about her welfare and wanted to do their best for her. Mr Talbot Cliff said Constance had done a silly thing, but they wanted to give her a chance. Constance would be bound over for three years on a surety of £5 on condition she went into a home and stayed there until they found her some work and accommodation.

Daphne Mumby was born in March 1932 and her earliest memory is of walking to school because it was a long way. She remembers going to a fancy dress party to celebrate the Coronation in 1936, dressed as a daffodil. The costume had been made of paper by her Aunty Alice. Daphne won first place and was given a doll.

Children didn't have many toys in those days and Daphne was delighted with her prize and used to play in the shed in the garden with it. At the time the family had a dog called Jack and one day when Daphne went to play with her doll she found the feet and toes had been chewed off. Her father wasn't very sympathetic telling her that Jack had probably thought the hands and feet were chocolate biscuits!

Daphne left school at 14 and went to work at the Appelby Frodingham Steel works in the office. She was there for nine years and met her husband Gerald when they worked in the same office.

In June the Medical Officer of Health reported that the population in the 1931 census was 33,961 and in the middle of the year had been about 33,990. The reason for the decline was the fall in the birth rate. The death rate had remained stable. There was an increase in deaths from respiratory diseases, but a decrease from infectious diseases like scarlet fever. The amount of benefits given out in 1931 had been £4,654, compared with £46,730 in 1930 and had been given to 86 men, 126 women and 180 children.

Winifred Todd was elected as Scunthorpe's Carnival Queen in July. She was crowned by film star, Heather Angel. Heather was born in Oxford in 1909 and after a short time on stage went to California. When she was 20 Heather was given a small part in the film *Bulldog Drummond*. In 1931 she had played the lead in *Night in Montmartre* and *The Hound of the Baskervilles*.

George Walker, a cobbler, had left Scunthorpe in 1852 and gone to America (Elgin, Illinois) where he subsequently made his fortune which he left to his daughter, Elizabeth. She died in 1918 and left £200,000 to the heirs of George Walker. In August 1932 a number of people in Scunthorpe with the surname Walker were keen to claim their share of the fortune. Claimants also came from several other areas including Hull, Rotherham and Bury. It looked as though one branch of the Walker family in Scunthorpe had been declared the rightful heirs after they appeared to have successfully established their relationship with George, until they received a setback. An American attorney stated that George Walker's daughter Elizabeth had in fact married a John Phillips and died thirty-five years earlier, so she could not have been the same Elizabeth to whom George had left his fortune. The Scunthorpe family were not prepared to give up though as they had evidence that George Walker had taken two daughters to America and that the attorney hadn't traced the other daughter. Meanwhile the fortune continued to sit in the bank and amass interest.

In September Marjorie Helena Goodhall was chosen as Railway Queen by a committee of artists from Liverpool, the first girl to be chosen from Lincolnshire. Marjorie, aged 14 from Sheffield Street, attended the Doncaster Road School and had left the Modern School in 1931. She was described by the newspapers as *a pretty girl with ringlets of dark hair and rosy cheeks* and delighted with the honour. Her father, G.W. Goodhall, was chairman of the local branch of the NUR and it was he who nominated his daughter. Marjorie had just started work as a clerk at the Co-operative Society in Scunthorpe. She was crowned at Belle Vue Manchester on 24 September by Mr A.G. Walkden, General Secretary of the Railway Clerk's Association.

Mrs Ivy Wilson lived next door to 49-year-old Ernest Parkhouse, an electrician, in Gervaise Street. On 11 October Ivy alleged in court that since 1928 Ernest had been threatening to tell her husband that she was associating with another man if she did not do as he wished. She also claimed that he had made two Dictaphone recordings of conversations she was supposed to have had with other men. Ivy stated categorically that she hadn't been with other men and reiterated that Ernest had been blackmailing her. Ernest denied all the allegations. The court decided there was insufficient evidence to proceed and the case was dismissed.

1933

In July, Mrs Peter Hannah, aged 30, of Ivy cottage, Yaddlethorpe Grange, near Scunthorpe was walking along the Scotter–Scunthorpe Road to catch a bus to take her to the maternity hospital, when she went into labour. Her husband, a labourer on the farm of R.B. Jones, (a magistrate), and her other two children were with her at the time. Fortunately, the weather was warm because although the police and ambulance were called, the baby arrived before they did. The ambulance arrived from Scunthorpe within ten minutes and found mother and baby in good condition. They took the family to the maternity home.

In front of a crowd of over 5,000 people on the Old Show Ground, Judy Kelly, the Australian born film actress, crowned Myfanwy Spink, aged 13 from Alkborough, Queen of the Scunthorpe carnival. On 20 July Myfanwy led the carnival procession. Judy went on to star in *Luck of the Navy* (1938), *Dead of Night* (1945) and *Dancing with Crime* (1947). The Carnival made nearly £1,500 for the hospital, which was a record.

Betty Cameron was born in 1933 and her earliest memory is of living at her grandma's house in Scotter Road. Betty went to Crosby School and she remembers the blackout and sirens going and endless queues. She also remembers being let out of school early to go potato picking at Alkborough. When Peggy left school she worked as a waitress. She then became a nurse and worked in the Scunthorpe Memorial Hospital and later at the Brumby Isolation Hospital.

On 23 July, the Scunthorpe police telephoned the Metropolitan police and asked them to stop a man who they believed had killed his wife and was on his way to London. Flying Squad men and Q cars patrolled the streets and every other policeman in London was on the lookout for him. Eventually the man was stopped in a lorry at Stamford. He declared his wife was perfectly safe and had left him at Retford after an argument and caught the bus back to Scunthorpe. The police checked the man's story and realised he was telling the truth. The wife was amazed that anyone should suspect her husband of murdering her. There had been a misunderstanding caused by the police's inability to understand the man's sister who was deaf and dumb. She had tried to tell them that her brother and his wife had had an argument, but they had not understood.

In August the town faced a serious milk shortage because of the hot dry summer. Many retailers had to ration their customers because there was little milk available locally and they were having to bring it in from places as far away as Uttoxeter.

Pauline Oats (née Metcalf) was born in Alford but moved to West Street in Scunthorpe when she was 6. Pauline went to the Doncaster Road Infants' School and then the Modern School in Cole Street. She began nursing at Scunthorpe War Memorial Hospital on 10 September 1933. At the time there were only sixty beds, nurses had to live in and weren't allowed outside in their uniforms. They could never run anywhere in the hospital except in cases of haemorrhage or fire.

Pauline recalls that patients having appendix operations were kept in hospital for ten days until it was time to remove their stitches and those having tonsils removed were fed with ice cream and toast. The day after the tonsil operation patients usually had stew for lunch and they would often joke it contained their tonsils.

By October there was still concern about rising milk prices. Milk now cost 7d a quart.

Rhona Stephenson, Scunthorpe's first carnival queen, was severely injured in a road accident on 26 September. Thomas Green, a butcher from Barnetby, Brigg, was driving towards Brigg when he collided with the car driven by Mr S.G. Stephenson of Winterton. The crash was so bad that both Rhona and her sister were thrown clear of the car and Rhona was rendered unconscious for several days. The prosecution alleged that Green had turned off with giving sufficient indication that he was going to do so. He was found guilty of driving to the danger of the public and fined £5 with £2 2s costs.

Mrs Lucy Hall was still matron of the Scunthorpe War Memorial Hospital when the new nurses' home opened in October 1933. The home had fifty-eight bedrooms as well as lecture, demonstration and sitting rooms, a study and a kitchen for teaching cookery for the sick. The building cost £15,000. On the day HRH Prince George, the Duke of Kent, opened the building, Mrs Hall told the nurses to wear cardigans under their uniforms because it was a wet day and she thought the prince would prefer to see the nurses smiling rather than shivering. He was the first member of the Royal Family ever to visit the town and thousands gathered in the streets to cheer and wave their flags when he arrived, despite the weather.

In November a Ministry of Labour official visited Scunthorpe looking for 500 female servants who could cook, to meet the growing demand in Leeds. During the summer several Scunthorpe girls had taken employment in holiday resorts but several more had applied for the positions in Leeds. Wages ranged from 15s to 19s with board and a room, which was more than the girls were being offered in Lincolnshire.

In the same month the Labour Exchange recorded that there were 1,221 people unemployed. Of these 932 were men and 289 were women. This was compared to a total of 2,168 in July and 3,000 the previous November. The steel works were busier than ever and the town was starting to feel more confident. By the end of the year the population of Scunthorpe had risen to over 35,000.

CHAPTER NINE

1934 – 1936

On 27 February at the Nottingham Assizes, nine Scunthorpe men were accused of offences against girls under 16. Three were acquitted and six were found guilty and sentenced. In his summing up the judge, Mr Justice Humphreys, stated that he wished he could also punish the girls too because as long as there was no means of punishing the girls as well these things would continue.

Arthur Allison, a 54-year-old steelworker was sentenced to nine months, William Chant, a 72-year-old tailor, was given six days which meant immediate release. Frank Warden, a 63-year-old

Frodingham 1934.

greengrocer was given six months in the second division, Arthur Alman, a 47-year-old caretaker was sentenced to five months in the second division, William Evelyn Cook, a 64-year-old slaughterman, received six months in the second division and George William Backhouse, a 60-year-old labourer, was given five months in the second division. All the men were convicted after admitting the charges or being found guilty by the jury of assaulting four girls under the age of 16.

Mr Justice Humphreys stated that two of the girls were around 13 or 14 at the time, but they had accosted the men and he was sorry he couldn't punish them as well.

The girls were taken to the juvenile court on 13 March. Two of the girls were bound over to their parents for £5 for two years. Another girl, a younger sister of one of the four who had not herself been involved in the original court case, was also in court because the police feared for her welfare. These three were sent to an industrial school, which was designed to help children who hadn't yet committed any serious crime but who needed to be removed from bad influences. At the school they would be educated and taught a trade.

The school timetable was quite strict. Children got up at 6 a.m. and went to bed at 7 p.m. During the day they received education, attended a family worship session, had meals and three short periods of play. There was also time to learn a trade. While the boys learnt gardening, shoemaking and tailoring the girls were taught sewing, knitting, housework and washing. Before the 1857 Industrial Schools Act, industrial schools were run on a voluntary basis. The Act covered children who were homeless but was updated in 1861 to include children apparently under 14 who were caught begging or homeless or whose parents couldn't cope with them, and those apparently under 12 who had committed a crime punishable by prison or less. The word 'apparently' was included because children might lie about their age. By 1870, the schools were under the responsibility of the Committee of Education.

The Co-operative Society was a large employer of single women in Scunthorpe. Once women married they would normally leave so they could look after their husbands and have children.

45 Old Crosby
Scunthorpe
Lincolnshire
17.3.34
To the Secretary, SCS

Dear Sir
On account of my forthcoming marriage I beg to offer my resignation
to terminate my employment with you on the 24th March 1934.

Yours truly
Kathleen M Parrott
(Dairy Dept)

Kathleen was born on 11 February 1911 to Percy and Lizzie Parrott (née Sleight) and married Ronald Taylor in March 1934. Kathleen died in October 1995.

Marjorie Millson, aged 15, was chosen as the Scunthorpe Carnival Queen in June, after a public ballot in which fifty-two town and district schools had entered candidates. Marjorie was crowned on 7 July, the day the carnival took place, by Lady Wormsley, wife of the Grimsby MP Sir Walter Wormsley. £2,000 was raised for the benefit of the hospital, which needed an annual income of £15,000 to meet demand and balance the books. The carnival procession was a mile long, stretching from Crosby to Brumby Wood lane.

Edna I. Towle was born on 10 July 1918 in Barton to Wilfred (b.27 February 1899) and Irene Towle (née Wood. b.16 June 1897). Wilfred served in the Royal Navy in the Great War and when he returned home the family moved to Scunthorpe. Edna was the oldest of five children. She had two brothers, Wilfred (b.1919) and Ken (b.1923) and three sisters, Barbara (b.1922), Joan (b.1926) and Brenda (b.1931). Edna was chosen to be the Queen Street Methodist Schoolroom May Festival Queen in May 1934.

By 1939 Edna was working as a spinner rope worker and living with her parents at 99 Butts Road, Barton. Her father was listed as a sloop master. Her brother Wilfred had also joined the Royal Navy, as an Ordinary Seaman on HMS *Archeron*. He died when the ship hit a mine off the Isle of Wight on 17 December 1940.

Edna married Charles Watkinson in 1942. She died in 2006.

In October, Elizabeth Olga Rowley Brooke, the daughter of W.J. Brooke, managing director of the Normanby Park Steelworks, appeared in court accused of driving recklessly at excessive speed in a manner dangerous to the public on the Brigg Road the previous August. She had been driving her mother's car home at 10.30 p.m. when she collided with a motor cyclist, Mr Cook, and killed him. Elizabeth pleaded not guilty.

The prosecution stated that Elizabeth had been driving at 45mph when she approached the junction of East Common Lane and had just overtaken a car without bothering to see if anything was coming the other way. Coming towards her was another car and although she swerved to the right she hit the offside of the approaching car. Elizabeth said the other car came out of nowhere and that she remembered jamming on her brakes but nothing else until she woke up on the grass verge. The other car hit three cyclists, killing the first one instantly.

The jury found her guilty of reckless driving and fined her £50. She was banned from driving for ten years and ordered to pay all the costs.

Brenda Todd (née Whitfield) was born in December 1934 in the maternity home that is now the Old Library on Trent Street. After the home closed the building became a museum and subsequently the library. One of her earliest memories was of lying in bed and wondering if the aeroplane she could hear flying over was German or British and feeling scared. She also remembers singing 'Ten Green Bottles' in the school air raid shelter and seeing a Spitfire flying over the playground. Brenda also recalls going to Station Road to see a house that had been bombed out.

Brenda was the first female ambulance driver in Lincolnshire in 1971 and she remembers the first ambulance she took out was so old it had a hole in the floor. The engine in another ambulance she drove would stop working if they went through a deep puddle.

1935

Margaret Mary Ashdown was born in Boscombe, Hampshire in 1896 to the Rev. Henry R. and Kate Ashdown (née Field). The

Bluebell Laundry girls 1935.

family had moved to Crosby by the time Margaret was 15 and the Rev. Ashdown became a well known vicar and social worker in the town. Margaret was a parochial lady worker by the age of 25 and living at 29 Cemetery Road. Later Margaret moved to Francis Street and became the organiser of the Brigg Division of the Conservative Association. Margaret became a member of Scunthorpe Urban Council in 1927 and president of Crosby and Scunthorpe Nursing Association. Early in the 1930s she moved to Lincoln to take up the post of secretary to the Lincolnshire Nursing Association.

Margaret died in March and her funeral took place on the 20th. Attending the funeral were the Earl and Countess of Liverpool, the MP for Lincoln Mr W.S. Lidall, the chairman of Scunthorpe Urban Council Mr D.J.K. Quibell, Lady Sheffield and J.F. Auld, clerk to the council.

Jean Simpson was born in March 1935 and remembers the feel and rubbery smell of her gas mask. Jean worked at the gas board when she left school and then became a nurse. She gave up nursing when she married Geoffrey, aged 19.

Maureen Naylor (née Houghton) from Barrow on Humber, remembers visiting her cousin in Scunthorpe regularly from when she was three years old in 1935. Her uncle managed the Jubilee Cinema and during the Second World War he also managed the British Restaurant in Scunthorpe.

Maureen's cousin would meet her at the station and take her back to the cinema for Saturday morning pictures. She always had a good seat at the front. During the war Maureen remembers an incendiary bomb dropping on her grandfather's outside toilet in Barrow on Humber. The visits to her cousin in Scunthorpe continued and after the war Maureen remembers watching Cornel Wilde in *Robin Hood* seven and a half times! Maureen also went shopping in Scunthorpe with her mother and then later, on her own.

In June, Clara Eastoe, a 20-year-old domestic servant from Dowse Avenue, bought a claim for damages of breach of promise against 21-year-old Arthur John William Frith, a shop assistant, of 10 Jackson's Road, Ashby.

In January 1934, Clara had slept with Arthur, something she wouldn't have done if she hadn't been sure Arthur was going to marry her. When Clara became pregnant she asked Arthur what he was going to do about it and he allegedly said that there was no need to do anything yet because it might not live. At the time Clara and

Scunthorpe Co-operative Society pre Second World War.

Arthur had been engaged to be married some time in August 1934 and Clara had already published the banns in Scunthorpe Parish Church, but in July Arthur had broken off the engagement without any reason. Clara told the court that Arthur had been a devoted lover and the break up had come completely out of the blue. In January 1935, Clara had given birth and had then been granted an affiliation order of 7s 6d per week. Although Clara had asked for £100 and £6 special costs, the court awarded damages of £75 with costs.

The Co-operative Society was seen as a good employer and any vacancies always attracted plenty of applications like these:

Dear Sir
I wish to apply for the situation vacant in the Boot and Shoe Dept.
I have attended the Scunthorpe Modern School for three years. I have been a member of the Co-operative Junior Chair for three years also.
Yours truly
Phoebe Beacroft
Age 15 years
Check No, 6864

Allenby Street
Scunthorpe
July 16th 1935

Mr A Wyld
General Secretary
Scunthorpe Co-operative Society
Dear Sir
Having seen your advertisement in the window I wish to apply for the position as stated for a girl in the Boot Department.
I shall be 15 years in October and have attended Modern School for nearly 3 years. I have also attended Mrs Ginn's night classes for 2 years and have gained the top position each year.
My parents Share No. is 8043
I remain, Yours truly
Audrey Joan Proudly

127 Berkley Street
Scunthorpe
13.7.35

General Secretary
Co-operative Society
Scunthorpe
Dear Sir,

Having seen the advertisement in the Emporium window for a smart assistant for the boot department between the ages of 15 and 16 years, I being 15 years, and 2 mths old, wish to apply for this position. I am attending the Scunthorpe Modern School, now being at the end of my fourth year, and I am anxious to find employment. My parents share number is 708. Trusting that I may be successful in my second application.

Yours faithfully
Nancie Tate

Audrey, Phoebe and Nancie were unsuccessful in their applications. In 1943, Audrey married Ronald Butler and Phoebe married Denis A. Wilson. In 1947, Nancie married William E. Robinson.

Annie Abel was born in 1900 in Hull to Robert and Hannah Abel (née Russell). She had three older sisters, Emily (b.1887), Ella (b.1888) and Jessie (b.1892), an older brother Robert (b.1894) and younger brother Edward (b.1901). On 21 June 1922, Annie married Maurice Roe at St Augustine's Church Hall but in September 1924 Maurice was killed in a motorcycle accident.

John Charles Williams worked for the Frodingham Ironstone Mines Ltd and lived in Frodingham Road. He met Annie in 1935 when she was living in Clarke Street. She'd told him her name was Annie Burton and she was a widow. On 21 September Annie, now aged 34, from Frodingham Road, married John Charles Williams at Crosby Parish Church and they began living together in Frodingham Road. The following month Annie appeared in court accused of bigamy – as she was already married to an Albert Poskitt from Hull. The couple had married on 19 April 1930 in St Steven's Parish Church, Hull and at the time Annie had said she was a widow and her surname was Roe. Annie had left Albert the following April and according to him, he'd seen nothing of his wife since. There hadn't been any children. Another witness said he'd known Annie since she was a child and in 1929 she'd told him her husband had been killed in a motorcycle accident and she was a widow. He'd attended her wedding to Albert.

Detective Sergeant Brewster told the court that when he had visited the property on 8 October Annie had admitted the charge. She said she'd left her husband because he was never at home.

On 6 December 1947, a 47-year-old woman by the name of Annie Poskitt was found in Lincoln with a razor blade and blood-stained handkerchief. When she appeared in court Annie, of no fixed abode, said she was a widow and pleaded guilty saying she no longer wanted to live and if they let her go she would make a proper job of it.

Kathleen May Cobban was born in Scunthorpe in 1903 to Alexander McDonald and Kate Ellen Cobban (née Rowbottom). Alexander was an architect and surveyor and the family lived at 188 High Street, Scunthorpe. Kathleen had an older sister Hettie (b.1902), a younger sister Margaret (b.1906) and a younger brother James (b.1910).

Kathleen was an assistant teacher at Scunthorpe Henderson Avenue School for twelve years before being appointed headmistress of Crosby Infants School in September 1935. She was also district captain of the Girl Guides, a member of the Juvenile Advisory Committee and superintendent of the Crosby Mission School.

1936

Norma was an only child and came to Scunthorpe when she was 2-years-old in 1936. Before that her parents had lived and worked on a farm in Burringham. She remembers her mother telling her that when her father came home with a white £5 note as his wages from his new job at the steel works, she had rushed off to the grocer's to check it was real as she'd never seen paper money before. On the farm Norma's father hadn't earned anything like that because much of the wages had been paid in milk, potatoes and sometimes the farmer gave each of his workers a pig.

When the first air raid siren went off, Norma was in Ashby library. She was told to run home as fast as she could, which she did but no bombs fell.

Norma also remembers that school didn't start until October in 1939 because the air raid shelters weren't finished. There were wooden huts between the infants and junior school and she recalls sitting inside singing 'Ten Green Bottles'.

Norma's mother wasn't well so Norma helped with chores around the house, scrubbing the outside toilet and the steps. Monday was washday. Although there was rationing they were never hungry or short of food. Her father kept a pig in the yard as well as chickens and Norma remembered the pig hanging in the yard with her father cutting bits off. Towards the end of the war she went shopping and joined a queue for fruit and vegetables that stretched down Market Hill and round several other streets.

Norma's mother's older sister had bought her up so when she came to stay Norma's mother wanted to make something nice for a surprise. Milk was rationed but she decided to make a semolina pudding. She made it, but it foamed up and didn't look right. Thinking the milk must have been off she remade the pudding, but the results were the same. Norma's mother had made three puddings and wasted three pints of milk before she realised that she had been using washing powder. The grocer would sometimes slip his customers a little extra in a blue bag and Norma's mother had thought it was semolina.

Norma started dancing at St Paul's Church when she was 7, but otherwise children made their own entertainment and cycled everywhere. She had a dart board and they did jigsaws as well. When she was 14 or 15 Norma thought nothing of walking to Bottesford to go to dances. They never had any trouble although Norma remembers that lads sometimes jumped out at them from the deserted army camp for a joke. Brassy Sharman, a tramp, lived at the army camp at that time.

When she left school Norma worked as a copy typist for the Ministry of Food, Agricultural Division in Cole Street. Norma met her husband when she went to a dance in the Corn Exchange in Brigg in 1952.

Vera Mary Walker of 43 Theodore Road married Basil Cox of 55 Trafford Street on 7 May. Both were members of a local wheelers' club and the bride was given away by her grandfather. They left for a tandem honeymoon, the bride dressed in plus fours, brown jumper, black velvet jacket, brown shoes and stockings.

In June, Sir Kingsley Wood, Minister of Health opened a new maternity home and stated that the death rate for under one-year-olds had been the lowest on record the previous year.

Christine Plumtree was born in July 1936. She was born on a farm and was the oldest girl so by the time she was 7 she could cook a three-course meal. She remembers walking 5 miles to school every day and back again at the end of the day. Christine was 14 before she tasted bought bread and butter because her mother always baked her own and living on a farm the butter was fresh. She was also 14 before electricity came to the farm.

Christine went to work in the kitchen at Normanby Hall when she was 16. She loved working there. In 1957, she married Kenneth and began working at the steel works kitchen. Her first breakfast was for 3,000 men. She remained at the steel works for twenty-five years.

In 1936, Scunthorpe became a municipal borough incorporating Ashby, Brumby, Crosby and Frodingham. The town had a weekend of celebrations and festivities, which included fireworks and concerts and displays by the band of His Majesty's Coldstream Guards, the

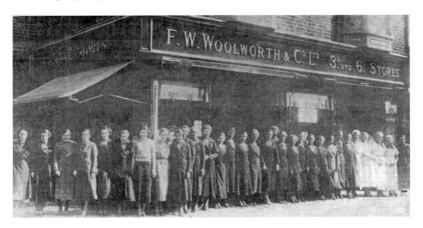

Staff outside Woolworths in 1936.

Hospital Carnival Queen 1936 Enid Baxter.

Scunthorpe British Legion and the Scunthorpe Male Voice Choir. While thousands lined the route of the procession through the town, crowds filled the Old Show Ground to see Sir Berkeley Sheffield Bart receive the Charter of Incorporation, created by Edward VIII, on behalf of the town from the Rt Hon the Earl Derby K.G. on 10 October 1936.

Shirley Binns (née Fish) was born in November 1936. Weighing only 2lbs, she was the smallest premature baby born at Brumby Wood Lane Nursing Home. There were no incubators at that time so they kept Shirley in the airing cupboard. She wasn't able to go home to her parents until the following April. Shirley's father was a builder who built lots of houses and he named Shirley Crescent after his daughter. When Shirley was 16 she worked in the Co-operative laundry until she married Peter in 1963.

Dorothy Lucy Trevena (née Bee) was born in December 1917, the daughter of Walter (1896 – 1962) and Ivy Bee (née Allison 1895 – 1972). She was the cousin of David Quibell, the town's MP for several years and later Lord Quibell. Dorothy was a former pupil of Messingham Primary School and the former Modern School in Cole Street, Scunthorpe.

Dorothy had wanted to be a nurse since she'd saved her father's finger at the age of 8 in 1926. He had been cleaning his motorbike when he almost cut off the end of his right middle finger. Dorothy had put his head between his knees, fetched some warm soapy water and washed his hand which was very greasy. After a long time and lots of water Dorothy stuck his finger tip back on and then bandaged it up. Over the next few weeks Dorothy did his dressings and the finger healed perfectly. In those days there were no antibiotics or anti-tetanus injections so it was amazing there was no gangrene.

Dorothy started work at Scunthorpe Hospital in June 1936 and reported to the matron's office. She was taken up to the children's ward where she met Nurse Belton who later became a good friend. Dorothy began by sluicing the dirty sheets before they went to the laundry. Dorothy spent the next three months doing this and was on the verge of giving up several times, but because they had to pay to be released from the probationary period, she stuck it out. By the end of the three months Dorothy realised she loved the job even though matron wouldn't allow her to go into theatre during that time because she did not think Dorothy looked strong enough. She was allowed to take patients to and from theatre though.

Dorothy was woken at 6.30 a.m. by the night sister to go for breakfast at 7.10 a.m. and her duties started at 7.30 a.m. These were to make the beds on one side of the ward and then pull them into the middle so the cleaner could sweep. She then replaced the beds in a completely straight line and dusted. The creases in the sheets and counterpane had to be lined up with the centre of the bed and the patient's nose. Pillowcase openings had to be facing away from the door and the lockers were in fixed positions. Matron often ran her fingers over tops of doors to check for dust. The rest of the day was spent washing patients, making beds, ward work and treating pressure points. Dorothy had one day off a week.

Dorothy married Donald H. Trevena in 1950. She died in 2010.

On 12 October, Mrs Kate Hornsby, of 120 Mary Street died. Kate had been the first woman councillor and female magistrate. Aged 74, Kate was the younger daughter of John Porkess of The Mill, Broughton. She was elected to the Brigg Board of Guardians in 1907 and the council in 1919. In 1920, she became a Justice of the Peace, and in September Kate laid the first brick of Scunthorpe's

£1,000,000 housing scheme, the first one in the country. She had also been a member of Advisory Committee of the Labour Exchange.

Kate had been the secretary of the Scunthorpe Women's Liberal Association, was a member of the County Maternity and Child Welfare Committees as well as a member of the War Pensions Committee and Board of Trade War Profits Appeal Tribunal.

On 15 November, Mrs Flora Alice Jarvis, a 52-year-old from 42 Francis Street, was rescued from Keadby Canal by two bargemen who pulled her to the side and lifted her out with boat hooks. They were on a Hull keel moored up at the lock when they had heard a scream and saw Flora struggling in the water. She was taken to the hospital, but other than shock appeared to be unhurt.

CHAPTER TEN

1937 – 1939

In February 1937, Mrs Doris Vanda Ursula Teesdale (née Woolsey) appeared in court accused of murdering her husband Cecil Walter Teesdale by shooting him with a revolver.

Doris was born on 20 March 1908 in Lincoln to Frederick Bishop and Elizabeth Sophie Woolsey (née Rawding). She met Cecil Walter Teesdale when he was working in Lincoln and they married in 1927. Cecil had a thriving butcher's business and the family were well known in Scunthorpe. The couple had been married for nine years and had one son, Anthony. Another son had died several years earlier. The marriage was volatile with Cecil spending considerable time out of the house and in the company of other women. He often boasted to his wife that he had kissed other women and Doris was lonely and depressed. During the summer of 1936, Cecil was known to have hit Doris on two occasions and in early December 1936 the maid heard a shot fired. The maid told the court that she was later shown by Mrs Teesdale where the shot had gone close to her husband's chair.

Doris explained to the court that she had complained about being scared when Cecil was out at night because they often had large sums of money in the house. His car was always parked outside when he was in, so it was obvious when he wasn't at home. Doris was concerned that if his car was gone she might be robbed. Cecil had shown her the gun and told her it was loaded with blanks. While he was showing her the weapon it went off accidently.

The couple had eaten Christmas dinner together and after the meal Cecil went to visit his mother. On Boxing Day, Doris had arranged a party but Cecil went out and did not come home until 10 p.m. The following day, 27 December, Cecil went out again. Mrs Teesdale asked her husband to take her with him, but he refused, telling her she was not broadminded enough. Doris went to bed about 11 p.m. expecting Cecil to be home by midnight. He did not return until 9.30 the following morning.

The maid said she could hear Mr and Mrs Teesdale quarrelling in the dining room, then she heard a shot followed by a crash and groans.

James Sanderson Vogwell, dental surgeon from Scunthorpe, told the court that he was telephoned by the maid who was very agitated. On his arrival at the house Mrs Teesdale told him that she had not meant to shoot her husband, only frighten him. Mr Vogwell said that Cecil was conscious when he arrived and had said, 'Look after her, it was only a blank'.

The Rev. Roland M. Thompson of Goole, Congregational minister, had been staying with Mr Vogwell and went with him to the house. When questioned in court he reported that Mrs Teesdale kept saying 'fetch the doctor, fetch the doctor, I didn't mean to do it'. Later she said to him 'I worshipped him but he has trodden on me. I never handled a gun in my life why did he have them about?'

Tom Fisher, another local butcher, set up a fund at the beginning of January to raise money for Doris's defence. He started collecting at the local cattle market and numerous people put in £5 or more.

On 10 February 1937, after two hours and ten minutes, Doris was found not guilty of murder and manslaughter by a jury of all men to wild cheering from crowds. She left court with her brother and father and went home to her son Anthony.

Doris remarried in 1938 in Blaby, Leicestershire to John A. Haines. She died in February 1992 in Leicestershire aged 83.

North Lincolnshire Red Cross Society was formed in March 1937 by Olive Nundy (née Black), Miss Harvey, Miss Friend and Miss Ivy Wilson. Other women included Miss Reynolds, Miss Benn and

Miss Henson. The group met in St Lawrence's Church Hall at first and then at the Youth Centre. During the war they reported to the centre during air raids, sometimes waiting for the all clear before going home and trying to catch a few hours' sleep before starting their day jobs. Olive worked at Firth Brown in Dawes Lane and was the first female first aider at the company. Olive left Scunthorpe in 1960 and moved to Cleethorpes where she joined the Red Cross for a short time.

Wendy Clark was born in July 1937. Wendy remembers being carried to the shelter at night wrapped in a blanket. She had two older sisters and they would creep back into the house when their mother wasn't looking leaving their mother frantic. Wendy remembers the feel of the gas mask and hating it because she felt like she couldn't breathe so she would rip it off. Her mother would say 'she'll be gassed!'. Wendy had no idea what that meant but she remembered it!

In October the Scunthorpe Employment Report showed unemployment down to a record low of 289 men compared with over 4,000 six years earlier. There was now a shortage of skilled workers.

1938

There was an outbreak of Diphtheria in February causing the death of a 5-year-old boy and his 6-year-old sister. Another twenty cases had been reported, mainly children, in the Ashby area. Brumby isolation hospital could not cope with the demand and several patients had to be taken out of the district, including the two children who died.

Doreen Redhead was born in 1938 and was a dinner lady for twenty-five years. Doreen loved working with children and during her spare time she was a volunteer with social services. Her friend visited parents who were struggling to cope and Doreen would go along and play with the children and then encourage the parents to join in. Doreen was also a member of the Methodist Church until it closed. In the street where Doreen lived all the houses had long gardens and she had a slide and a sand pit and was always full of children who called her Aunty Do.

On Saturday, 26 March, an SOS was flashed across all the cinema screens in Scunthorpe for Miss Margaret Weatherby.

Kiosk at one of Scunthorpe's cinemas.

Staff of ABC Cinema pre Second Word War.

Her fiancée, 23-year-old Aircraftsman George Morgan, had left Scunthorpe on the 19th after finalising their wedding arrangements for Easter. He had gone back to his RAF base in Felixstowe,

Suffolk and been taken ill. He was now in Ipswich hospital with cerebral meningitis. Margaret and George's parents were found and the three drove all night to sit by George's bedside, but he sadly died on Sunday 27th.

Because they had been in contact with George, his parents and Margaret were kept in isolation and not allowed to go to his funeral. Margaret's sister attended, as did George's brother and various aunts and uncles but, because of the cause of death, the Scunthorpe Medical Officer would not allow the coffin in the church. The coffin lay on an RAF lorry covered in wreaths while the service was held and his colleagues from the RAF stood to attention with reversed arms.

Kathleen Elaine Singleton, aged 15, of Priory Lane, Ashby worked at Rapid Cleaners in the High Street. She was adjusting some clothes in the window in May when her right hand was caught in some machinery. The machine was stopped as soon as other workers in the shop realised what had happened and they called for help. Two doctors and a mechanic arrived and were soon trying to free the girl. In the meantime a large crowd gathered outside to watch. Inside the window the electric fan was switched off and fumes built up causing Kathleen to pass out and making those trying to free her ill. One of the doctors had to smash the window to let the fumes out. Kathleen was trapped for over half an hour before they were able to free her and then she was taken to Scunthorpe hospital suffering from shock and with a badly crushed hand. In 1944, Kathleen married David M. MacMichael.

On 6 June, 3-year-old Frank Stephenson was playing on the banks of the River Trent near Derrythorpe with another child, a girl, when he fell in. His mother, Mrs Elsie Stephenson, a 30-year-old farmer's wife, couldn't swim but after being told by the little girl that her youngest child had fallen in she jumped in anyway. Fortunately, her feet touched the bottom and with the water up to her neck she reached the spot where her son had fallen in, but all she could see was his beret. Somehow she managed to grab him just as he was sinking and struggled to the bank where neighbours helped them out. Elsie was almost near collapse and Frank needed artificial respiration but both recovered.

In 1938, Joyce Miskelly applied for a job with the Co-operative Society in the Dairy Department. Joyce was born at the end of 1922 in Goole, Yorkshire.

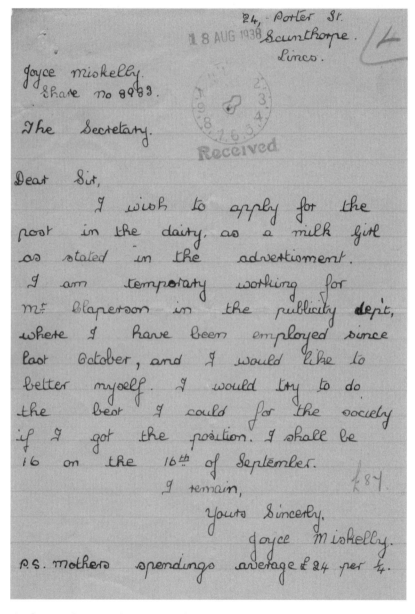

Application Letter to Co-operative Society.

THE SCUNTHORPE CO-OPERATIVE SOCIETY LIMITED.

T   E   S   T.

ARITHMETIC.

Attempt Question 1 and three others.

1. Add the following:-

£.	s.	d.	
-	15.	11	23041
-	13.	10	740999
1.	17.	$1\frac{1}{2}$	87878
-	2.,	9	97979
-	3.	$1\frac{1}{2}$	34215
-	12.	6	652576
-	4.	7	418490
-	9.	9	30857
-	8.	5	893939
-	6.	6	
3.	14.	2	
-	8.	8	
-	14.	9	
1.	17.	7	
-	16.	8	
-	4.	3	

2. Find the value of 16 boxes of soap, each box contains
    half-a-cwt. at $2\frac{1}{2}$d. per lb.

3. What must be added to 45 times 8010 to make 55 times 8012?

4. If 63 pence weigh 1 lb. 9 ozs., what will be the weight
    of a guinea's worth of pence?

5. What number must be added to 1,000,000 to make it exactly
    divisible by 492?

ENGLISH.

Write down the feminines of tiger, hero, bull, marquis,
uncle, nephew, bridegroom, abbot;
and the plurals of commander-in-chief, penny, echo, solo,
ally, choir-conducter, lord-justice, cuckoo, chimney.

Application test for Co-operative society.

Having secured an interview Joyce then had to pass an arithmetic and English test. Joyce passed with 150 out of 150.

21st September 1938

Miss J Miskelly
24 Porter Street
Scunthorpe
Dear Madam
With reference to your interview with my Board, I have decided to advise you that it was decided, subject to you passing an Approved Medical Examination, to offer you the position in the Dairy Department.

Your wages for this position will be at the rate of 6 and 1/2d per hour, with a guaranteed minimum of 35 hours per week.

The appointment is on the understanding that the Society does not guarantee you employment after attaining the age of 17 years.

I shall be glad if you will kindly call at my Office, in order that arrangements may be made for the Medical Examination.

Yours truly
General Secretary

To ensure Joyce was fit for employment she endured a rigorous medical examination, had her height (5 feet 1 inch), weight (7 stone 7 lbs), chest (32 and a half inches), waist (23 inches) measured and her heart and pulse rate checked. Her eyes were examined to see if pupils were equal and reacted to light and whether her reflexes were correct to ascertain whether her nervous system was normal. Her teeth and gums were checked, urine samples were examined and the doctor made sure she did not have any signs of venereal disease or anything else that could cause her to be unfit.

30th September 1938

Miss J. Miskelly
24 Porter Street
Scunthorpe
Dear Madam
Further to your interview with my Board for a position in the Dairy Department, I now have pleasure in advising you that you were

successful in passing the Approved Medical Examination, and therefore, confirm your appointment to this position.

Kindly advise me when you will be able to commence your duties.

Yours truly
General Secretary

Joyce married Ephraim J. Graves in 1942.

In September 1938, Gladys R. Elsome also applied for a job with the Co-operative Society. Gladys was born on 21 August 1921 to Milton Edwin and Edith Annie Elsome (née Norton).

Wells Street
Messingham
Scunthorpe

Dear Sir,
I am writing in answer to your notice for a female for the Messingham milk-round.

I am 17 years of age and our Share No. is 5829

Yours truly
Gladys R. Elsome

To get the job Gladys had to first pass the arithmetic and English test and then the medical examination.

7ᵗʰ October 1938

Miss G. R. Elsome
Wells Street
Messingham
Dear Madam
With reference to your application for the position of Milk Roundsgirl at Messingham, I now have pleasure in advising you that you were successful in passing the Medical Examination, and therefore confirm your appointment to the position.

You will commence your duties on Monday, the 10ᵗʰ instant, at 6.30 a.m. Our Mr. A. Smith, Outside Supervisor, will arrange to see you at No. 16. Branch premises at the time stated.

Yours truly
General Secretary

In 1939, Gladys was unmarried and living with her father, an iron foundry furnaceman, mother and unmarried sister Doreen who was an uncertified teacher. Gladys was still a milk rounds girl doing heavy work. She died in October 1992.

In October, 10-year-old Jean Hogg, daughter of Mr and Mrs Fred Hogg of 41 Diana Street, was rushed to hospital with tetanus. She'd cut herself a week previously and the cut appeared to have healed but then she was taken ill. The hospital immediately injected 150,000 units of anti-tetanus serum but the infection was too far advanced and Jean didn't respond. Scunthorpe hospital didn't give up. They sent to London for some more anti-tetanus serum and a car raced to Scunthorpe from London with 1 million units of the serum. It was injected as soon as it arrived, but again there was no sign of improvement, in fact the signs were that Jean was approaching death. Despite the fact that no other child had ever recovered from being this ill the staff injected her again and then there was the faintest sign of improvement. The hospital had injected over 1,000,000 units of serum now and gradually Jean began to recover. Jean was the first child ever to have recovered after developing tetanus within seven days of being injured. By the 21st of the month Jean was back home and her parents overjoyed that their daughter had survived.

Eleanor Joyce Featonby, aged 28, from The Oaks, Appelby met Thomas Welch of Newcastle in Seahouses in 1936, when they were both there on holiday. The couple became close very quickly and not long after Eleanor returned home Thomas came to the house she shared with her parents and stayed for a few days. As they were waiting for his train back to Newcastle, Thomas, an insurance officer who was in the TA, proposed to Eleanor and she accepted. Thomas gave Eleanor an engagement ring, Eleanor gave Thomas a cigarette case and their engagement was formally announced. The marriage was due to take place in 1937, but Thomas was ill so it was postponed until 1938. Eleanor was an elocution teacher and an amateur actress but knowing she could not continue with these once she married, she gradually stopped both work and her amateur dramatics.

The couple corresponded regularly while they were apart and in one of these letters Thomas insisted his sister came to live with them after they were married because she hated the idea of having to go into digs.

Eleanor was not at all keen on that idea because she and Thomas's sister, Miriam, did not get on and had become involved in several quarrels. When Eleanor explained that she didn't want Miriam living with them because of this Thomas became annoyed. He explained that Miriam was like a mother to him and the only way he was going to share a house with Eleanor was if Miriam came and lived with them. Thomas blamed Eleanor for the arguments, saying she had feelings of enmity and loathing towards Miriam and that all the time his sister was single her wellbeing was his priority.

Eleanor tried to be conciliatory, suggesting they meet to discuss the matter rather than keep bombarding each other with letters, but Thomas refused, saying Miriam's welfare was his priority and that

Brumpton's Lemonade pre Second World War.

Eleanor should now release him from his engagement because the rift was irrevocable.

Eleanor refused and when he failed to go ahead with the wedding Eleanor took him to court for damages. Eleanor was awarded £25 and Thomas was ordered to pay costs.

In December, the Women's Voluntary Service (WVS) formed a branch in Scunthorpe and within a very short time ninety-two women had enrolled.

CHAPTER ELEVEN

The Second World War

1939 - 1941

In 1939 Scunthorpe was allowed to adopt its own Air Raid Precaution scheme, the only borough able to control its own ARP. By January the number of women in the WVS had more than doubled. Major Lewis, ARP Officer for Scunthorpe, told a public meeting that he had received many representations from women in Scunthorpe who wanted to take more part in ARP. Of the 182 WVS women doing a variety of duties, 73 covered First Aid, 7 were ambulance drivers, 7 were general transport drivers, 22 were working in canteens and catering, 6 were working in the care of children and another 24 were involved in miscellaneous tasks. There were 22 ARP Wardens

Family in Exeter Road building their air raid shelter.

and 18 involved in other duties. However, Major Lewis stated that it was not enough; 200 ARP wardens were needed and extra women were also required for auxiliary services, evacuation and the care of children. Two women had been sent to Barton on Humber for the LAGC course. They were the only two Scunthorpe women to take the course and they passed out at the top.

In February, the Lincolnshire National Fitness Committee and Lincolnshire Women's Recreation Association held a meeting in the Vicarage Rooms in Scunthorpe and discussed the provision of more outdoor sport for women and girls in the district. Alderman H.V. Tombs presided over the meeting and said that the county committee felt they should start some form of outdoor recreation for the women of Scunthorpe. They decided that when the corporation's new park or playing fields became established provision would be made for netball and other games as well. The meeting decided to form the Scunthorpe and District Games Association, which would include a netball league with two divisions, one for juniors, the other for seniors. One of the physical trainers, Miss Fox, explained that the object of giving the organisation that particular name was so it could include hockey, rounders and women's cricket in the future.

The Co-operative Society was still the major employer of women in the town and on 4 February Olive M. Roberts applied for a position.

> *44, Haig Avenue*
> *New Brumby*
> *Scunthorpe, Lincs*
> *4.2.39*

Dear Sir,
On seeing your advertisement for girls in the Dairy Department I wish
to apply for the post.
I am seventeen years of age. Share No. 6866
I am Yours faithfully
Olive M Roberts

Olive managed 50 per cent in both the arithmetic and English test.

1st March 1939

Miss O M Roberts
44 Haig Avenue
New Brumby
Scunthorpe
Dear Madam
Further to your interview with my Board regarding a position with this Society, I have pleasure in advising you that it was decided to offer you a position inside the Dairy Department.

Your wages for the position will be at the rate of 5d per hour, with a minimum of 35 hours a week.

The appointment is subject to you passing an Approved Medical Examination, and if you will kindly call at my Office, arrangements will be made for your Medical Examination.

Yours truly
General Secretary

Olive went on to pass her medical examination too and duly started work.

Olive Horne, aged 16, was enjoying her temporary employment with the Co-operative Society and was encouraged by her supervisor to apply to be a permanent member of staff.

132 Frodingham Road
Scunthorpe
5.2.39

Dear Sir
I wish to apply for the vacancy in the dairy dept. I have already been working there since November temporarily, but was told by the supervisor to apply. I have been working outside and like the work very much.

Yours faithfully
Olive Horne

Her application was accepted on 1 March and she was offered 6½d per hour for a guaranteed minimum of 35 hours a week.

In April there was a meeting for National Service held in the cinema. The mayor of Scunthorpe announced that the Home Office had given Scunthorpe permission to buy thirty steel air raid shelters which would each accommodate fifty people. If necessary, they could be erected very quickly in streets off the main shopping centres of the town. In addition, the council had been given permission to build fourteen underground shelters which would also accommodate fifty people per shelter.

Miss M.E. Walker, Woman's Voluntary Service Regional Organiser who had driven an ambulance in France during the First World War, also spoke. She addressed the women present and stated that the women of Scunthorpe had the honour of being the only women in Lincolnshire or Yorkshire to outnumber the men in their district in voluntary service. However, the 219 volunteers currently involved was just the beginning as in the

Air raid shelter 1939.

next three years they needed to double their numbers. She was sure they could achieve that as it was vital for the country that they succeeded. She also told those present that their other duty was to get every man they thought should volunteer and take him to the National Service office in the High Street and see he got on with the business.

At the beginning of the war men were called up and the women took over their jobs. Edna May Goodhand of Moorwell Road, Yaddlethorpe remembers there was a signal woman at NP North box. Edna started at Winteringham as a porter, working with others. Mr Bartlett was the stationmaster at Winteringham and he passed Edna as a porter/signalwoman. She was then sent to operate the box at Winteringham. The train that was known as 'the special' was a priority potato train and there was also a covered platelayer's trolley with two seats at the back. The platelayers walked along the line hammering the blocks on the track. The gangers were Fred Hawkins and George Armstrong.

After a while Edna was sent to Whitton as a porter on her own. The goods here were mainly potatoes and hay. Edna loaded the 14lb bags of potatoes onto the empty wagons by herself. No coal trains/wagons came into Whitton from Winteringham or Winterton loaded. Edna helped sheet the wagons, the goods would arrive at the station, Edna would load them and then the train would leave.

Edna lived in West Halton and cycled to work at Whitton, arriving before eight o'clock. The farmers hired sacks from the LNER for their corn. These were sent to the farmers, filled and tied in bundles of twelve. The coal for the station fireplace came from the goods locomotive. Edna's husband's uncle was one of the drivers at Markham, another was a man called Jonty Spence who gauged the wagons. Edna remembers a farmer at Whitton, Spillman, loading a large number of potatoes on a train which was short of wagons. There were too many sacks for the train so it wouldn't pass under the gauge. The sacks had to be unloaded and the remainder sent the next day.

At Winteringham four Scammell lorries moved a hundred tons of cement per day from the South Ferriby cement works but none of the coal that came into Winteringham was for the cement works, it was all for local delivery.

The only train per day to Whitton usually arrived in the afternoon. It was nearly always empty when it arrived, but full when it left. Covered vans also arrived at Winteringham for the cement traffic. The cement came in 8-stone paper bags. If the cement was still hot it would make the handlers' fingers raw. The cement was also sent out in jute sacks which resulted in a short strike by staff until the loaders received masks and overalls. The NUR men came down to support the staff but the women did not belong to the union and were not asked to join in the strike. At that time there were five or six female staff at Winteringham. The foreman was Bill Cowling from Alkborough who was too old for the forces. Edna didn't do much paperwork as a lady called Laura Barley did most of that.

Edna worked from 8 a.m. to 5 p.m. and was paid between £3 and £3 10s a week. When the porters had spare time, they played cards in the waiting room. Edna rarely saw the management other than when there were problems, as with the strike.

Whilst at Winteringham Edna couldn't recall ever seeing any vessels at the pier along the Haven line that were not in use. There were also sailing ships still in use on the Humber. Later Edna worked at Thealby where Mr French was in charge. He'd requested Edna to work there. She did not have much to do with signalling at Thealby but remembers there were rabbits everywhere. Edna was the only woman porter there and had some good laughs, but she had to shut her ears to the language!

Although the war finished Edna stayed on until 1950.

Ann Grey was a parlour maid with the Brook household when war broke out. Frederick Gough was manager of Lysaght's Normanby Park Works and he chose Ann to head the female workforce. Ann was the first woman on the works and the morning she started she remembers the eyes of 3,000 men watching her. Ann did several different jobs around the works to prove women could do them and soon she was joined by several other female employees. Ann recalled that when the air raids started the men rushed to the shelters while the women stood staring up at the sky and had to be hustled into the shelters.

Dorothy Unwin from Kenilworth Road also recalls the women going into the canteens rather than the shelters when the air raids took place. Dorothy did several jobs in the works starting in the mill counting the slabs as they went through the cutter. She then went to the blast furnace where she hauled sand and clay as well as oiling and greasing the wagons at the sinter plant.

Marion Taylor of Axholme Road was 18 when she worked as a hot saw checker in the 15-inch mill.

Women also manned the overhead cranes, welding, machining, coil winders, paint girls, diesel loco drivers, anything that was within their physical capabilities.

Marion Smith was 15 when the war started. She joined the Civil Defence as a messenger, recalling that twelve or fifteen of them used to be in the air raid shelter (where Naylor's the undertakers is now). If the telephones were bombed the teenagers took messages on their bikes to air raid wardens. Marion remembers that not long after she began as a messenger they were taken to the old show ground (where Sainsbury's is now) and taught to take a Sten gun apart, clean it, put it back together and fire live ammunition.

Maureen remembers listening to Lord Haw Haw one night on the radio. He'd said that Scunthorpe had been flattened, but other than some fire bombs on the steel works and the bathroom hanging out of a house in Station Road that had been hit, the only thing that had been killed was an animal in a field, either a cow or horse.

Maureen worked in a shoe shop for a while, then when she was 17 she joined the buses as a clippy. The buses took the US airmen back to their bases. Maureen worked until 11 p.m. and then walked home in the blackout. She remembers Scunthorpe was full of different nationalities including Poles, Canadians and Americans, but she never felt unsafe or had any problems. Maureen then volunteered for the YMCA. They had a dance floor where the forces used to go and Marion made teas there and was taught to jive by the Americans.

Maureen: 'If you saw a queue you joined it even if you had no idea what they were queueing for'.

Maureen's boyfriend worked in the steel works at first but then he went to work in the foundry in Lincoln where they made tank tracks. He later volunteered for the RAF and flew Lancaster bombers. He was shot down on his thirteenth mission and ended up as a PoW in Stalag Luft 3, the camp where the Great Escape was planned and executed. When he came home he and Marion married. Marion's uncle fought in Burma and her husband's brother was in North Africa with the Desert Rats.

By September, the women of Scunthorpe had responded to the appeal, issued on behalf of the Scunthorpe Hospital Linen Guild, for workers to provide supplies for the Red Cross, St John Ambulance services and the Scunthorpe Hospital. Mrs N. Varty, one of the signatories of the appeal, said the response to the appeal had been extremely good with those women who were unable to take part in other activities volunteering in great numbers. Women who wanted to take part in knitting or making bandages, dressings and other things were urged to get in touch with Mrs Varty, 7 West Cliff Gardens or Mrs W.B. Baxter, WVS Organiser, 34 High Street, Scunthorpe. Work could either be done for the Red Cross or Scunthorpe Hospital. Women who were unable to take part, but who still wanted to help could become a member of the Linen Guild by paying a subscription of 2s 6d or more or by making donations for the purchase of materials for the Red Cross.

138 Sheffield Street
Scunthorpe, Lincs
November 15th 1939

Dear Sir
Having worked inside the Co-operative Society temporarily since 10th July 1939 I wish to apply for a permanent situation.
   My age is 16 years and my parents share number is 10286.
   Hoping this application will meet with your approval.

I remain, Yours faithfully
Gertrude Reilly

9th December 1939

Dear Miss Reilly

Further to your interview for a position with this Society, I have pleasure in advising you that it was decided to appoint you to a position in the Dairy Office when Miss Andrews leaves the employ of the Society.

Your wages for the position will be 11.9d (eleven shillings and ninepence) per week.

If you will kindly attend at my Office at your earliest convenience, arrangements will be made for your Medical Examination.

Yours truly
General Secretary.

32 Dale Street
Scunthorpe
Lincs
24.11.39

Dear Sir

With reference to your advert for a dairy assistant I wish to apply for the situation. I am seventeen and a half years of age and am present employed as a domestic servant.

Yours faithfully
(Miss) Jean Nicholson
Share Number 2693

9th December 1939

Miss J Nicholson
32 Dale Street
Scunthorpe
Dear Miss Nicholson

Further to your application for a position in the Dairy Department of this Society, I have pleasure in advising you that, subject to you passing an Approved Medical Examination, your application was successful.

Your wages for the position will be at the rate of 6½d (sixpence halfpenny) per hour, with a guaranteed minimum of 35 hours per week.

If you would kindly call at my Office at your earliest convenience, arrangements will be made for your Medical Examination.

Yours truly
General Secretary

1940

Patricia Stephenson was born in 1940, the youngest of three sisters. Patricia was left-handed and she remembers the teacher hitting her hand with the ruler to make her use her right hand. After this happened several times Patricia's knuckles were raw and when she hid her hand from her father he wanted to know why. Patricia explained and her father visited the school; after that she didn't have any trouble.

Patricia went to Saturday morning pictures from the age of 7 and was a member of the ABC Minors. It cost 6d to get in and they watched whatever was on. After she'd left school Patricia began work at the office in the steel works where they had just installed a massive computer. One unit of the computer was big enough to fill the whole of St Paul's Church Hall and Patricia had to go to Berkshire to learn how to use it. Later she worked with social services. Patricia had never forgotten her father telling her that she should always vote because women had died for her to have that right.

Patricia met her husband when she was 17 and he was in the RAF completing his National Service. The couple married when she was 20 and he was 21. Patricia loved dancing although her husband wasn't so keen, so they went to the cinema a lot.

On 15 March, Lindsey County Council's Education Committee reported that the headmaster of Scunthorpe Grammar School had objected to the medical officer's woman assistant examining boys. The committee replied that they saw no reason why girls and boys shouldn't be examined by a woman doctor and that the examinations would go ahead.

In April, nurses at the Brumby Isolation Hospital hung a child's gas mask outside the window of a girl who was suffering from a serious illness. A dove from the hospital dovecote used to fly over and sit on the windowsill outside the girl's room, but as soon as the child's gas mask was placed outside she moved in, and at Easter laid two eggs. The girl's health began improving once the dove started visiting her and the matron was hoping nothing would happen to disturb the doves before the eggs hatched.

In July, 25-year-old Elizabeth Marie Borchardt, a German citizen from Philip's Crescent, Scunthorpe, was arrested in Hampstead

Road, London. At Marylebone Police Court on 31 July, she was charged with being out after curfew. Elizabeth smiled nervously at the magistrate, R.L. Dunn, and explained that she was on holiday in London from Scunthorpe for a few days and staying at Hillfield Court, Belsize Road, Hampstead. She had been out with a gentleman friend and forgotten the time. Elizabeth was fined 20s and told not to let it happen again.

On 1 August 1940, King George VI and Queen Elizabeth visited Scunthorpe. This was the first visit by a reigning monarch to the town.

Mrs Dorothy Glover (née Symonds), a 40-year-old widow from Messingham Road, Ashby, was taken to Sheffield hospital in August. Dorothy had tried to kill herself twice since July and told her brother, William Symonds of Bottesford Road, Ashby, that she would never go home. On 5 September, Dorothy disappeared from the hospital in her nightdress, dressing gown and slippers. Despite an extensive search, there was no sign of her. At the end of the month Elizabeth's body was found in the River Trent, 40 miles from the hospital. The police told the inquest they were trying to trace her movements and work out how she'd travelled so far.

1941

By the beginning of 1941 the population of Scunthorpe had risen to over 48,000.

Ivy Doreen White was a domestic servant in Scunthorpe and aged 17 when the court found her guilty of stealing a purse containing a ten shilling note and 1s and 3d in money from a dance hall. Ivy had already been on probation twice, once for stealing two handbags and the second time for theft in Otley. The courts heard how Ivy had been led astray by her mother, a convicted receiver who'd been to prison twice and who'd been given a six-week sentence for receiving the 10s note. Ivy's father was a good hard-working man but her four brothers had also been led astray by the mother. According to the probation service, three of the boys had been sent to Borstal and the other to a home in Lincoln and, away from bad influences, were doing very well. The probation service further stated that Ivy was dance mad and

Clover milk delivery.

needed discipline. Ivy was sentenced to Borstal for a period of not more than three years. On hearing her sentence she collapsed and had to be carried from court by a prison officer.

Clara Gregg, aged 62, wife of James Gregg of Bushfield Road, was born in Bradford and then lived in Rotherham for some time before moving to Scunthorpe. Clara had been an active worker for the Soldiers' Comforts Funds since the outbreak of war and was known as 'mother' to many soldiers. Clara collapsed and died suddenly at the end of January and at her funeral in February six soldiers were coffin bearers. Another party of soldiers, including a major, also attended and saluted at the graveside.

Scunthorpe started a Youth Service Corps in March to help women and older people. Sixty girls and forty-six boys from Scunthorpe Grammar School signed up for the Corps initially and many more volunteered after the first meeting. Some of these were chosen to go to the town's council estates and offer help to women whose husbands were away in the forces with gardening, carpentry, painting, minor electrical repairs and looking after the children.

On 15 May, Scunthorpe Women's Voluntary Services put out a statement saying there had been reports of women going from door to door begging clothes saying the WVS had refused to help them. The Scunthorpe organiser, Mrs E.M. Howatt, assured residents that the WVS would never refuse to supply clothes to needy applicants and she asked anyone who was approached by women begging should speak to the local WVS office as soon as possible.

In June Susanna Liddall from 82 Mary Street died aged 87. Originally from Swineshead, Susanna was the widow of Benjamin Liddall and mother of Lincoln MP, W.S. Liddall.

On 29 July, councillors and members of the public at the monthly meeting of Scunthorpe Council were taken by surprise when a smoke bomb filled with sulphur was thrown into the room, the doors were locked and the lights went out. It was part of an ARP exercise and was carried out to show the advisability of always carrying a gas mask. Unfortunately, many councillors had left their masks in the cloakroom and some members of the public had not bought theirs with them. For ten minutes chaos reigned, women fainted and others were convulsed with coughing. The councillors were not amused, especially as some thought that other members had been warned and so were able to put on their gas masks and laugh at the discomfiture of their fellow members. They passed a motion stating their strong disapproval at the ARP action. A month later the council withdrew its motion of disapproval.

The North Works canteen at Scunthorpe Steelworks was opened in September 1941. The management had decided that steel workers should have a canteen that was open twenty-four hours a day so they could obtain hot meals during all shifts. The management did not forget their women workers and mess rooms were built at Frodingham, Appleby steelworks and South Works.

At the North Works canteen Mrs Syvret was employed as cook assisted by Mrs Coulson and Winnie Wheatley. Peggy Neil and Doreen Howell supplied the meals over the counter. Brenda Smith was the tea girl and Margaret Marshall and Joan Burkhill washed up. Joan Stringwell was the vegetable girl.

In 1941, No.1 Canteen cooked 6,609 meals and served 29,573 beverages; No.2 Canteen prepared 4,463 meals and 7,549 beverages; No.3 Canteen 2,103 meals and 4,761 beverages. Frodingham mess room served 10 meals and 846 beverages, Appelby 125 meals and 1,652 beverages and South mess room 19 meals and 222 beverages. The canteens employed 60 people, mainly women.

In September the parents of Scunthorpe began complaining to the Education Board about the lack of school places for their children. All building of schools had stopped when the war started but parents pointed out that even before the war Scunthorpe had a young population with a high marriage and birth rate and they blamed the Education Board for not planning properly. Overcrowding in schools was rife, as was the lack of male staff to take the more senior classes.

In November the Scunthorpe Women's War Work Depot, which represented all the women's voluntary organisations in the town, announced that they had despatched over 17,000 garments to hospitals, prisoners of war and members of the Armed Forces since the war began. Nearly 10,000 of these garments had been made in the previous year and 2,177lbs of wool had been knitted into these comforts. Lady Sheffield stated that the Central Hospital Board had been delighted with the quality and speed of the work, especially the two rush orders, gloves for prisoners of war and hospital garments for Russia.

CHAPTER TWELVE

1942 – 1944

On 6 January, Margaret Mary Davis, daughter of the late Mr and Mrs J. Davis of Aldenham, Watford, married Alan Heseltine, son of Mr and Mrs A. Heseltine of New Brumby. Margaret wore a white French net dress with a headdress and orange blossom and a full-length embroidered silk veil. She carried a bouquet of white lilies and maidenhair fern. John, her brother, gave her away. The four bridesmaids were Margaret's cousins, Lily Moore and Jean Ellis, and Alan's nieces, Thelma Heseltine and Sheila Campbell. Apart from Lily, who wore a pink and black net dress with a matching hat, the bridesmaids wore pink dresses and headdresses and carried

Grocery delivery.

bunches of anemones. Horace Campbell, the bridegroom's brother in law was the best man.

A new Red Cross ambulance was presented to the town in January. Most of the money to pay for the ambulance had come from Mrs Fanny Johnson who left the charity £500 in her will.

Betty Doreen Hunsley, aged 19, appeared in court on 26 March accused of murdering her 5-month old son, Eric. Betty was single and a factory worker and she lived at 57 Burringham Road, Ashby. She had been stopped by police at the junction of Rowland Road and Brigg Road and taken to Scunthorpe police station. After speaking to her, police went to the girl's home and in the air raid shelter of the back garden they found Eric's body. Betty was remanded in custody.

On 11 June, Betty appeared in court and told how they'd been sleeping in the air raid shelter at night. She'd covered Eric with a rug and he looked warm enough. Betty had checked Eric several times in the night and he'd been all right but then, when she woke in the morning, she had discovered that he was dead. Betty said she was so frightened she had hidden the body under the seat. Betty was found not guilty.

Mrs Ellen Stevenson married in April 1941 and moved to 24 The Close, New Brumby, Scunthorpe from Barnoldswick. Almost exactly a year later at 11 a.m. Ellen was alighting from a bus having been shopping. She walked around the back of the bus, and whilst trying to avoid a car coming towards her she failed to see a lorry. The driver swerved but was unable to avoid Ellen. The inquest accepted there was nothing the driver could have done and the verdict was of death by misadventure.

Married women were struggling to find part-time work in the town partly because of the lack of co-operation by employers and partly because there were few opportunities being offered. In April, Scunthorpe Employment Advisory Committee appointed a special sub-committee to investigate more avenues for part-time work and to seek more help from employers.

The Scawby Women's Institute continued to meet during the war. The ladies met in the hut in the centre of Scawby. Several women from the WI looked after evacuees during the war.

In July, Lindsey County Council approved the appointment of policewomen. The Police Committee approved one attested patrol driver and two attested policewomen for Scunthorpe for patrol and enquiry work. Mrs M. Winteringham asked what they meant by 'attested' and was told that although the women would have the same powers as men it was unlikely they would have to use them. The chief constable went on to explain that they had taken their best female civilian employees and they had already been trained up in the Metropolitan area.

In the same month, the Scunthorpe War Work Depot reported they had sent a further 1,038 woollen articles to the forces and 1,638 to the Red Cross in March, April and May. Since the war started, Scunthorpe's women's sewing and knitting groups had supplied 24,880 items.

1943

In 1943 – 1944 Scunthorpe had its first female mayor, Councillor Mrs Ada Eyre JP. Ada received the Freedom of the Borough on 8 March 1966 in recognition of a long and distinguished record of public service with a special interest in the field of education.

Councillor Mrs A Eyre 1936 – courtesy of North Lincolnshire Council.

Susan Marritt's grandmother, Alice Hind, was born in 1890s and grew up on a farm in Ashby, where the Sunshine Hall is now. It was later subject to compulsory purchase by the council. Alice was a nursing sister in the Great War where she met Ernest. The couple married and after the war Alice worked at the Rowland Road Hospital. Susan's mother Pauline grew up on the farm and went to Ashby School. She was also a nurse and in 1943 she met James who was in the Royal Tank Regiment. James had been badly burnt in North Africa and he was a patient in the hospital.

In January, two married sisters, 27-year-old Lily Spikings of 16 Bushfield Road and 29-year-old Winifred May Peatfield of 5 Haig Avenue, appeared in court. They were charged with stealing a number of small items and a clothing coupon book. The women had been spotted by an undercover policewoman on 21 December. Mrs Spikings was also charged with using two clothing coupons which had not been issued to her or to a person on whose behalf she was acting for the purpose of purchasing a pair of stockings. Mrs Peatfield was also charged with transferring a clothing coupon book. They both pleaded not guilty.

Eva Pacey, an auxiliary policewoman, explained to the court that she was on duty in plain clothes when she saw the two defendants take Christmas cards. Mrs Peatfield also took a book, some packets of Christmas seals, a lace collar and two rubber gas pipe fittings. The women left the store and were stopped by Police Constable Farman. At the police station the goods were found in their possession. PC Farman, who was also working in the store in plain clothes, corroborated Eva's evidence. Having listened to the evidence both sisters changed their plea to guilty.

Chairman of the Bench, Alderman J. Tomlinson, stated that this kind of offence seemed to be growing and that there did not seem to be any financial reason for either woman to steal. They were fined a total of £5 each and both ordered to pay 5s 6d costs.

Mary Catherine Harrison (née Adams) was married to Ernest Frank Harrison who owned Glanford Motors in Brigg. They sold up and moved to Scunthorpe where they started Enterprise and Silver Dawn. The company had several female bus employees during the war, including Mary who drove American and Canadian service men, who had been out of town, back to their bases. They normally had a military policeman on board in case of trouble. One night Mary was driving up Sawcliffe Hill under shrouded headlights when she had a feeling something was wrong so she slowed down. This was fortunate because a few yards further along there were Canadian troops on the road carrying out night manoeuvres. Mary carried on driving for the rest of the war and went on to drive double-decker buses in 1949.

On 2 January 1943, the Spitfire Fund reached its target of £5,000, which was enough to pay for one of the fighters which was named 'Scunthorpe'. One of those who helped raise the money was Florence Spooner who organised dances at the Crosby Hotel. The band was from Hemswell Airfield.

Mary Ann Gleadle was born in Blyton in 1854 to Thomas and Louisa Gleadle (née Manders). Thomas was a foreman. She had a younger sister Harriet (b.1856) and five younger brothers, George (b.1858), Thomas (1860 – 1867), William (b.1862), Charles (b.1865) and Thomas (b.1868).

Mary married Samuel Morely, a labourer, in 1874 and moved to Scunthorpe. The couple had six children: John (b.1875) Charlotte (b.1879) Sam (b.1882), Louisa (b.1884) Annie (b.1887) and William (b.1889) before Samuel died in 1890.

Mary married Samuel Ball in 1894. Samuel already had a son, Herbert Ball (b.1884) from a previous marriage.

Mary Ann was living at 14 Lygon Street when she died in May 1943, aged 90. Mary had thirty-one grandchildren, sixty-eight great grandchildren, many of whom lived in America, and two great-great grandchildren. Mary Ann had been knitting comforts for the Red Cross and Old Brumby Soldiers Fund right up until her death. She was one of the oldest members of the Old Brumby Church.

In September, Councillor and Mrs G. Stanley Atkinson, (Sheriff of Hull and his wife) attended the Mayoress of Scunthorpe's toy fair in aid of the Merchant Navy Fund in the Trinity Methodist School room. The sheriff praised the loyalty and work of the men and women of Scunthorpe, saying their work was greatly appreciated in Hull which had experienced the force of the enemy's bombing. He paid tribute to the Merchant Navy and said thousands of Hull men owed their lives to them. Councillor Atkinson specifically mentioned Donald Owen Clark who had been posthumously awarded the George Cross for helping to row his lifeboat out of danger and cheer his comrades, despite very severe burns. Mrs Ada Eyre, the mayoress, said the fair had already raised £374 for the fund and her aim was to raise £4,000. The Queen sent two dolls to the fair and a Polish doll was sent from Edinburgh.

1944

Barbara Joan Elliot was born on 27 August 1930 to Bill and Ethel Elliot and lived in Ashby Road. She left school at 14 and began work for the Co-operative Society Dairy in Roland Road in 1944. Barbara worked with the horses delivering milk on the Priory Estate

Bus worker during Second World War.

in Ashby. When she first started she was a driver's mate and went in the lorries delivering milk to the steelworks canteens. The milk was in 12 gallon churns, which were very heavy to load and unload. When the weather was really bad Barbara sometimes started at six in the morning and did not finish until seven or eight at night. The Co-op used to teach their employees to drive and at the age of 17 Barbara passed her test and then took out her first vehicle, a large old coal lorry. Drivers were rewarded for safe driving and given medals for five and ten years and gold bars for the intervening years. Barbara received twelve gold bars and two medals, leaving the Co-op because of ill health, just before she was due to receive her third medal.

Barbara married Arnold Richards in 1955. She died in 2005.

Christine was born in 1944. Her earliest memory is moving to Bottesford when she was 4-years-old and starting school. The huts had a big chimney in the middle and were very warm. She remembers one Christmas they made paper baskets and their teacher, Mrs Hunter, placed the bags on the top shelf. Just before Christmas they were given back their bags and they were full of sweets. Christine was convinced the fairies must have filled the bags. She remembers these as being the best years of her life. 'Everyone was so friendly, the women used to sweep the paths and then lean on their brooms and chat'.

As she grew older she remembers the fields had brown single-decker buses which the cows used for shelter. She and her friends would take a jam sandwich and some water and go and sit in them and pretend they were their own homes. Christine doesn't remember noticing at the time but she's pretty sure now that the buses must have smelt awful!

Nora Hanley worked at the Hibaldstow Radio Location Tower as a logger in the winter of 1944. Her job was to log all communication in a large ledger. Shifts ran from 8 a.m. to 12.30 p.m. and from 12.30 p.m. to 5 p.m.

The structure was well fortified from the outside, but on the inside there were only two WAAFs with a rifle. There was no ammunition and no instructions on how to use it. The building was in the shape of a hexagon with the instrument in the centre and a wheel showing the points of the compass. When the pilots spoke over the radio the operator turned the wheel to the compass point where the pilot was. Once she was sure she was correct the radio operator depressed the wheel and a signal would confirm or refute her computations. She would then give the pilot his bearings. The door was kept locked and bolted at all times. They received deliveries of paraffin for the stove via Motor Transport and the Elsan toilet was emptied every week by the sanitary wagon. The girls picked up their tea, cocoa, milk, sugar, bread, margarine, cheese rations from the cookhouse every evening and bottles of water from a tap at the bottom of the garden. Their furniture consisted of two chairs, a swivel office-type chair for the operator and an ordinary one for the logger. There were blankets for when there was no flying and the floor was covered in brown lino which was highly polished so it passed the occasional inspections.

The snow in February and March 1944 was so heavy the girls were cut off and unable to be relieved for two days so they were left with no option but to raid the farmer's potato store and cook them on the stove with melted snow because they'd run out of water.

CHAPTER THIRTEEN

1945 – 1950

1945

Ivy Murphy was a land worker. A female ganger would be telephoned by the estate or farm and she would come around in a lorry to pick up the women. There would be a dozen or more waiting for work. Ivy's son Terry remembers there were four houses to a yard with one tap and an outside toilet that the council emptied at night. Everyone did their washing on a Monday but because all

Staff at Scunthorpe Hospital 1940s.

the houses used coal fires, soot would soon cover the clean white sheets. He also remembers the ATS using the school playground at nights and weekends to practise their drill.

On VE Day the families hung the bunting up to celebrate the end of the war in Europe and to get ready for their street party. Masserellas, the ice cream company, came around the houses. Unfortunately, the cart had a large ice cream cone on top and it caught on the bunting and pulled it down.

> *White-House*
> *Gunness, Scunthorpe, Lincs*
> *May 26th 1945*

Dear Sir

I wish to apply for a situation in the grocery Dept.

I am 19 years of age, and have had three years experience in the Grocery Dept. of Pontefract Industrial Co-operative Soc. Ltd South Elmsall Branch.

I have a reference from the Secretary and Gen Manager of same.

> *Yours Faithfully*
> *M.L. Walter (Mrs)*
> *Stamped received 28th May 1945*

> *1st June*

Mrs M.L. Walter

White House

Gunness

Scunthorpe

Dear Madam

Further to your interview, I have to confirm your appointment to a temporary position in the Society's Grocery Dept.

Your wages for the position will be 27/-d + 17/6d Bonus per week.

Kindly arrange to report for duty on Tuesday, the 5th June, 1945, to Mr. J.W. Clark, Central Grocery Department. Please bring with you your Health and Unemployment Card.

> *Yours truly*
> *General Secretary*

Helen Marjorie Ramsden was awarded an MBE in the Birthday Honours List in June 1945. Helen had been the Training Officer of the Women's Voluntary Service for seven years and was the secretary of the Scunthorpe and District National Savings Committee. Prior to the Second World War, Helen had been the chairwoman of the Brumby Unionist Association. She had an MA from Newnham College Cambridge and had been a member of staff in the Pupil Teachers' Centre in Scunthorpe.

With the end of the war men were returning and looking for employment. Women who had been employed by the Co-operative Society were now surplus to requirement. The following letter went out to nine women, including Mrs Edna Hookham. The other recipients were Mrs A. Robson and Mrs L. White from No.14 Branch; Mrs O. Grunter No.15 Branch; Mrs Florence Pearson No.12 Branch. Mrs M. Moore and Mrs S. Proctor kept their positions in No.10 Branch, but Mrs E. Foley was made redundant. Mrs E. Allison and Mrs L. Robinson from No.4 Branch and Mrs Norah Cranidge from No.2 Branch also received the letter.

29th November 1945

Mrs E Hookham
No. 17 Branch
Crosby Avenue
Dear Madam
With the return of the permanent members of our staff, the question of temporary staff has been under consideration and in view of the nature of your position with the society, it has been decided to dispense with your services. This will take effect as from Saturday, December 8th 1945.

I am desired to convey to you the very sincere thanks of my Directors for your help and assistance during a very difficult and trying time. My Society have been particularly happy in the choice of yourself as an employee, and the best wishes of everyone goes with you on your relinquishing your position with the Society.

Yours truly
General Secretary

With their husbands returning home other women chose to leave.

> Butterwick Road
> Messingham
> Scunthorpe, Lincs
> Monday 10th Dec. 1945

Dear Sir

Please accept this my resignation as shop assistant. I am now employed at No 16 Branch in the Grocery Department, and the reason for leaving is to take up household duties, in readiness for my husband returning from the Forces.

    I am hoping to be able to leave my employment on the 22nd December and I trust you will accept this as my final notice.

> Yours truly
> M Wheeler (Mrs)

> 12th December, 1945

Mrs M. Wheeler
Butterwick Road
MESSINGHAM
Scunthorpe
Dear Madam

Your resignation of the 10th December, 1945, to terminate your employment with this Society on the 22nd December, 1945, was submitted to my Directors and accepted.

> Yours truly
> Assistant Secretary

> 100 Reginald Road
> Scunthorpe, Lincs
> 12/12/45

To-: Mr Auty
General Secretary

Dear Sir, I beg to give notice from Dec 15th to terminate my employment with your society on Saturday 22nd owing to the fact that I am expecting a baby in the near future and my husband will be out of the army.

> Yours faithfully
> N Dale (Mrs)

20.12.45

Dear Sir

I wish to give notice of my resignation from your employment on 25th Dec in order to take up a career of nursing. Will you therefore please accept seven days notice as from the date above included.

Thank you

I remain yours truly
Miss R Wood

14 Ashby High Street
71 Berkeley St.
Scunthorpe, Lincs
5/1/46

Mr Auty
Dear Sir

I wish to hand in my resignation to terminate on the 12th January. The reason being my husband is now demobbed and wishes me to be at home.

Hoping this will be accepted.

Yours truly
Mr F. Bowers

All the ladies received a brief note saying their letters had been submitted to the directors and accepted. Others were leaving to join the Armed Forces.

17 Messingham Road
Ashby, Scunthorpe, Lincs

Mr Auty (General Secretary)
The Scunthorpe Co-operative Soc. Ltd
Dear Sir

I have been accepted in the Womens Royal Navy, and therefore wish to tender my resignation. My services with the above society to terminate Saturday Feb 2nd 1946.

Yours faithfully
A Brumpton

Unknown WRN.

1ˢᵗ February 1946

Miss A Brumpton
17 Messingham Road
Ashby
Scunthorpe
Dear Madam
Your resignation of the 25ᵗʰ January, to terminate your employment with this Society on the 2ⁿᵈ February 1946, was submitted to my Directors and accepted.

They desire me to thank you for your past services and trust you will be happy in the Services.

Your truly
Managing Secretary.

Miss M Naylor
12 Victoria Road
Ashby, Scunthorpe, Lincs
25/1/46
Dear Sir
I have been accepted for the WRNS and wish to terminate my employment with the Society on Wednesday Jan 30ᵗʰ 1946.

Yours faithfully
M Naylor

The Princess Street families and the street decorations.

VE Day Princess Street.

Miss M. Naylor received the same reply as Miss Brumpton.

Elsie Mitchell, aged 31 of 7 Queen Street died of acute peritonitis after a swab was left inside her following a Caesarean operation at the Scunthorpe Maternity Home. The coroner said the death was caused in part by a lack of preparation by the theatre sister and the gynaecologist should also bear some of the responsibility. The inquest recorded a verdict of death by misadventure.

1947

In March the Trent Valley flooded and over a thousand children from Henderson Avenue School were unable to attend school while the authorities used the school to accommodate people from nearby villages who had been cut off by an 18 mile lake. The WVS helped the police bring in the evacuees and organised clothing collections for the flood victims.

In April 1947, there was a smallpox outbreak in Scunthorpe with eight cases being reported. It was also decided by the Borough Council in April to make chickenpox a notifiable disease. In November the children's ward was closed in Scunthorpe Hospital after five babies died within ten days after an outbreak of gastroenteritis.

In the early 1950s, women found work in Riley's Potato Crisps Ltd, which began producing crisps full time in a small warehouse in Allanby Street. The firm had been started by steelworkers, brothers Alfred (Biff) and Dennis Riley in 1947.

Isabelle was born in Trafford Street and had several brothers and sisters. She worked in Cotto's who made washing machines and this was where she met her husband. She also worked in Barton, making bicycles and in Riley's.

Linda O'Conner (b.1948) was and still is a great fan of Scunthorpe United. Her earliest memory is of her father taking her to watch them play when she was 5-years-old. She remembers the lovely meat pies, wonderful atmosphere and Kevin Keegan who used to play for Scunthorpe before he went to Liverpool.

June Fell (née Gray) lived with her aunt and uncle after her mother died. Her uncle was an air raid warden and June remembers going to the Henderson Road school with her gas mask. She then went to the Scunthorpe Technical School and from there she began working in a shop. She met her husband Ray when she and her friend joined the TA. They were married fifty-eight years.

1949

On 19 January, the public gallery at Scunthorpe's Magistrates' Court was packed with women when Mrs Hilda Green, a 41-year-old housekeeper, was charged with murdering 14-year-old Joan Mason. Joan, who lived with her widowed father Herbert in Scunthorpe, was found dead with head injuries outside her home on the night of 15 December.

On 28 February, Mrs Green appeared at Nottingham Assizes and was escorted into court by two policewomen. As she sat in the dock she took notes. Mr J.F. Claxton, prosecuting, outlined the case. He began by saying that Mrs Green had been given notice to leave her employment at the time of the girl's death. At 8.30 a.m. on 15 December, Joan and her friend Katherine Ulyett, who lived nearby, took their bicycles to school. Katherine Ulyett told the court that when Joan went to school she was wearing a black and tweed check coat and nothing on her head apart from a red ribbon. At about 12.15 p.m. Joan left school to go home. Another girl waited until 1.10 p.m. for Joan but she didn't re-appear so the girl went back to school without her.

Between midday and 1.15 p.m., Mrs Green was seen in the back garden of the house hanging out washing and one of the items on the line was a blue and yellow scarf which belonged to Joan. The next time the scarf was seen was when Joan's body was discovered, the scarf lying between the dead girl's forehead and her arm.

Joan's father, a steel worker, arrived home from work just before five o'clock and found the house in darkness. When he went into the scullery he noticed the floor was wet as if it had been washed. Mrs Green was in the sitting room and informed him that Joan had not been home for dinner and she was worried the girl might have been abducted. When Joan still hadn't come home Herbert went around to see Kathleen Ulyett and when he came back he saw Joan's body lying outside the scullery door. Mr Caxton said the prosecution thought the body had been dragged to the scullery from an open recess at the back of the house because blood had been found on the topsoil, as had plaster casts of five footprints which matched a pair of shoes Mrs Green had been seen wearing that afternoon. The police also found the box containing Joan's Christmas presents covered in blood.

Mr Caxton explained that Joan had asked her father for permission to draw one pound from her savings book. Mrs Green was there at the time. When Mr Mason checked the book he discovered that someone had been forging it.

After speaking to Scunthorpe Savings Bank the police discovered that on 14 December, someone calling themselves Mrs Mason had withdrawn ten pounds from the book.

On 1 March, Mrs Green was found guilty of murder and sentenced to death. Her execution was fixed for 30 March at Strangeways Prison. On 9 March she was given leave to appeal which was rejected on 25 March, however, on 6 April the Home Secretary recommended a reprieve.

Betty York of Scunthorpe married Prince Wladyslaw Cytartoryski in Switzerland on 28 January. The couple met when they were patients at the Montana Hall clinic. The Polish prince was now a British citizen.

Elsie Celia Peck was born on 17 November 1924 to Edward (b.1893) and Elsie Peck (née Bradshaw, b.1897). Edward had worked at the steel works since 1907 and could remember handling hot ingots with steam cranes. In 1939, Celia was a millinery assistant and living with her parents at 97 Rowland Road. By 1950, Celia was employed in the Plate Mills working with the preheater furnace. Her brother Ted was a driller in the Central Engineering Works.

In 1949, Celia married George Tom Bones (1919 – 1980), a burner in the Plate Mills. Tom's sister Dorothy was a paint girl on the 10ft Bank at the Plate Mills and was previously an overhead crane driver. Her husband Sidney Robinson, known as 'Shotty', was a loco driver.

After Tom died in 1980, Celia remarried James R. Knipe. She died in 1984.

In November it was reported that four or five student nurses a week were leaving Scunthorpe Hospital because of restrictions placed on them by matron after a few nurses had climbed up the fire escape to get back into their rooms. The students said that their lunch time break had been cut from three quarters of an hour to half an hour and their midday cup of tea stopped. The nursing home doors were now locked at 9.15 p.m. instead of 11 p.m. and their breakfast in bed privilege on their day off had been stopped. Another nurse complained that even if you were over 21 you had to write home to get your mother's permission to have a late pass and these were now restricted to two a week and nurses still had to be in by midnight. The fire escape had been sealed and two prefects had been appointed to go around each night to ensure all windows were fastened.

Matron Miss Vera Allen explained that most of the student nurses were only 18 and 19 and that she couldn't permit girls coming in at 2 a.m. or 3 a.m. by way of the fire escape and then cooking chips in the kitchen, using all the fat ration and then leaving the mess for others to clear up. Lord Quibell, Chairman of the Management Committee said they were aware of the situation and had told matron to tighten up discipline.

In December there was success for Dorothy Munnings in the Pontefract Open Table Tennis competition. Dorothy won the girls' singles and P. Skerrat and Kathleen Peake were runners-up in the mixed doubles.

The Legacy

Since 1950, women's lives in Scunthorpe, like those in the rest of the country, have changed considerably. Almost all the morals and norms that governed women's lives no longer apply. But have women's lives improved?

Women in this country now have the vote and a legal right to equality, so for those in most sections of our society the answer is an unequivocal yes. Contraception is freely available, abortion is now legal and women are no longer stuck in an endless cycle of childbearing. Infant mortality rates have fallen considerably since the early 1900s and up until recently some of the worst childhood diseases had all but been eradicated. Labour-saving devices in the home, freezers, vacuum cleaners, supermarkets and equality of household tasks have all helped to give the majority of women more control over their lives.

In most sections of society women can report domestic violence and have a reasonable expectation that they will be listened to and the perpetrator prosecuted. Women have equal access to further education, they can wear the clothes they choose, have their own bank accounts and credit cards and they are no longer considered the property of their father, husbands or other male members of the family. They do not have to put up with rape, sexual discrimination or harassment. In fact, the number of people getting married has fallen, with many couples choosing to live together instead. Having a child out of marriage is now perfectly acceptable and women are no longer forced to give up children for adoption because they're not married, nor are they made to give up work once they marry or became pregnant. It is considered normal for women with children to have a career although some may still struggle to be accepted in a few industries and professions. In theory women also have a right to equal wages although this is still a work in progress in some institutions.

But have these changes given women a better quality of life? My answer to the question is probably yes. I say probably because one of the things many of my contributors mentioned, although I didn't include it in their sections, was the lack of respect in today's society. The women I spoke to, and the newspapers I trawled through in my quest for stories, indicated that women appeared to be much safer in the wider community prior to 1950 than they are now. Although domestic violence was quite prevalent, attacks by strangers were relatively rare. This may be because rapes and assaults were less likely to have been reported, or because people lived in smaller communities and everyone knew each other, but it could also be that men's attitudes to women were different. Whilst female equality should not be seen as a threat, extreme feminism has alienated many men. Violence against women continues both inside and outside the home and is not helped by those who seek to make women more than equal to the detriment of men.

Despite legal equality there are still sections of society that persist in trying to reduce that hard fought for equality by portraying women purely as objects for sexual gratification. Certain elements of the media continue to put women under pressure to conform to some unrealistic ideal and others deliberately concentrate on women's physical attributes rather than view their achievements in the same way they would those of men. Other members of society are stuck in the Dark Ages and still consider women as inferior beings to be owned and controlled.

When the suffragettes originally fought for equality there were other women who thought they were wrong and that women shouldn't have the vote. This attitude still prevails today albeit in a different form. There are now women who are intent on removing women's right to choose how they earn their living and how they dress. The important words here are that it should be a *woman's right to choose*, and that if that choice is forced on them by men or other women then it is not choice. Denying women the right to choose how they live is not compatible with equality and is not what the suffragettes fought and died for.

Female equality, like every other aspect of our lives, is subject to many differing opinions including a school of thought among some feminists that the pressure on women to have it all: a career, children and a happy marriage/partnership has only increased the pressures women face in their everyday lives, rather than reducing them. Whatever your views, there is little doubt that the lives of women in today's Scunthorpe would be completely unrecognisable to Elizabeth Borman and her draper's shop in 1846.

Scunthorpe Steelworkers Sculpture by Ray Lonsdale, commissioned by the Scunthorpe Steeltown Team and unveiled on 3 November 2018.

The base reads:
Dedicated to all past and present steelworkers and their families from Scunthorpe and the surrounding areas. For those who spent their working lives keeping the steel production flowing through the Second World War. To their contribution to the war effort, the British economy and to the building of this town. To those who were injured or lost their lives in service on the steelworks. This is a debt that can never be repaid but will never be forgotten.

Bibliography/Sources

Appleby Frodingham News

Armstrong, M. Elizabeth, *An Industrial Island: A History of Scunthorpe* (Scunthorpe Borough Museum and Art Gallery, 1981)

Hull Daily Mail

Lincolnshire Chronicle

Lincolnshire Echo

Scunthorpe Evening Telegraph

Women of Steel (The Foundation for Wellbeing, 2008)

Ashby Salvation Army

Helen Marris Collection: Co-operative Society material and Scunthorpe Church of England School

Bryan Longbone

Eddie Baker

Maureen and Kevin Hempsall

Ancestry

Find My Past

Forces Records

Index

Jones, Ida, 99
Jubilee Cinema, 116

Keadby, 3, 124
Keegan, Kevin, 166
Kelly, Judy, 108
Kemps, Kathleen, 67
Kennington, Florence Eliza, 101
Kent, 88, 109
Kent, Winnie, 66
Key, Gladys, 58
Killick, Police Sergeant, 91
King, Mrs, 33
Kings Lynn, 57
Kirk, Ernest, 48
Kirk, George, 42, 48
Kirk, Harold, 48
Kirk, Thomas, 47
Kirk, Percy, 48
Kirton-in-Lindsey, 44, 55, 99
Knipe, James R., 169

Labour Exchange, 73, 110, 124
Laird, Margaret, 21
Lancashire, 29, 87, 97, 100
Lanely Street, 86
Langton, Nellie, 67
Lark Hill, 77–8
Laughton Forest Home, 55
Ledger, Thomas, 92
Leeds, 72, 110
Lees, Robert, 2
Liddall, Benjamin, 149
Liddall, Susanna, 149
Liddall, W.S., 149
Lincoln, 3, 12–14, 20, 42, 54, 58,
  62, 90, 99, 115, 119, 125, 144,
  147, 149
  Assizes, 24
Lincolnshire, 2, 9, 14, 22, 26, 30,
  39, 54, 68, 79, 81, 88, 100, 102,
  113–15, 126, 138, 140, 153, 172
  Echo, 96

1st Regiment, 35, 44
1/5th Regiment , 48
6th Regiment, 39, 48
Lindsey County Council, 29, 60, 67,
  79, 105, 146, 153
Lindsey House, 51
Lindum Street, 95
Liverpool, 29, 115, 166
Lloyd's Avenue, 97
London, 14, 38, 51, 57, 68, 71, 86,
  87, 92, 103, 108, 134, 147
Longbone, Bryan, vi, 172
Luck of the Navy, film, 108
Ludgershall, 38
Lupton, Florence Edith, 69
Lygon Street, 23, 155

MacMichael, David M., 129
Manchester, 82, 97, 107
Manley Street, 16, 52, 70, 73
Manger, Enid, 67
Markham, Enoch, 2
Markham, Mrs, 40
Marris, Helen. Collection, xi, 172
Marshall, Ellen, 19
Marshall, Hannah, 64
Marshall, Margaret, 149
Mary Street, 15, 26, 40, 123, 149
Marwood, Constable, 89, 98
Marwood, Mrs, 98
Mason, Joan, 167
Mason, Kathleen, 66
Masserellas, 160
Maternity Home, 73–4, 108, 114,
  121, 166
Mathy, Kapitanleutnant Heinrich, 40
Mennell, Elsie Jane, 31, 44
Mennell, Thomas, 73
Mesopotamia, 97
Messingham Road, 85, 147,
  163, 165
Methodist Church, 4, 6, 32, 127
Middelmiss, Phillis May, 75